THE NECESSARY REVOLUTION

IN AMERICAN EDUCATION

The
Necessary
Revolution
in American
Education

by FRANCIS KEPPEL

HARPER & ROW, PUBLISHERS

NEW YORK AND LONDON

To Deedie,
who paid the price

Acknowledgments

I have had the opportunity to think out some of the ideas reflected in this book in earlier papers. Some of the questions discussed in Chapter VI, "Quality in Education: The Teachers," were explored in the 1961 Horace Mann Lecture, "Personnel Policies for Public Education," published by the University of Pittsburgh in 1961. Some of the discussion in Chapter IX, "The Need for Leadership," was developed in the First Annual Alfred Dexter Simpson Lecture on Administration, "Public Policy and School Administration," April 28, 1961, published by the New England School Development Council in 1961. Those familiar with my reports as Dean of the Harvard Graduate School of Education will find there echoes of other thoughts expressed in this book.

Colleagues in the U.S. Office of Education, former colleagues at Harvard, and friends made in the course of twenty-five years in education have helped to form the views that have gone into this book. But the final result is my own responsibility. Friends deserve thanks, not blame.

F. K.

Contents

[ix]

APPENDIX A

APPENDIX B

Charts and Tables

Preface

One useful purpose of a preface is to state what a book is *not*. This book, then, is not an attempt to treat of all of the major problems in American education. It deals, for example, with the schools, and not, except peripherally, with the colleges. Nor is it a text for use in colleges or universities. In fact, educators will find themselves impatient with its review of many questions long familiar to them.

My main intent in *The Necessary Revolution in American Education* is to reach American laymen, for education concerns them deeply and they are often troubled by the complexities of the issues about which the educators speak. Education is the business of the American people, and this book is an interim report on the state of a part of that business. It can only be interim, because the wheels of American education are revolving so rapidly that whatever stability we had in the past is gone forever.

In the enthusiasm of becoming a grandfather for the first time, I recently said that my grandson's generation would be able to handle mathematics and the basic ideas of science far more effectively than mine. He will read faster and remember more. He will have learned far more of other lands and other peoples. He should be able to handle another language with ease, and it might well be a non-Western language. He will be better able to move from one kind of work to another during his lifetime, for the changes in our society and in our educational system will mean that he will have to have a better basic education, and therefore a better ability to apply himself to new jobs and new ways of life. Stability for him will include intellectual change.

But the education of our grandchildren will depend for its strength and its flexibility upon *our* ability to transform the American system of education so that the promises of equality of opportunity and the promises of high-quality education implicit in the democratic ideal are fulfilled. This book discusses some of the obstacles to the fulfillment of these promises, and some possible ways to overcome them. It makes no effort to cover all the topics of concern to citizens or educators today, but rather puts its focus on the national concern with elementary and secondary education in terms of the American tradition, and on certain issues of public policy affecting the schools. It tries to provide up-to-date information on some new developments and trends.

If this book stimulates concern for the welfare of the schools and the society they serve, it will have fulfilled its purpose.

F.K.

THE NECESSARY REVOLUTION

IN AMERICAN EDUCATION

1 The Necessary Revolution

The first revolution in American education was a revolution in *quantity*. Everyone was to be provided the chance for an education of some sort. That revolution is almost won in the schools, and is on its way in higher education. The second revolution is *equality* of opportunity. That revolution is under way. The next turn of the wheel must be a revolution in *quality*.

Since the word "education" has many meanings, it is necessary at the start to define it within the context of this book. Of the classic studies of education, one looms above its fellows: Werner Jaeger's *Paideia: The Ideals of Greek Culture*. In the introduction, "The Place of the Greeks in the History of Education," Jaeger has proposed the following definition:

Every nation which has reached a certain stage of development is instinctively impelled to practise education. Education is the process by which a community preserves and transmits its physical and intellectual character. For the individual passes away, but the type remains. . . . As man becomes increasingly aware of his own powers, he strives by learning more of the two worlds, the world without him and world within, to create for himself the best kind of life. . . . Education, as practiced by man, is inspired by the same creative and directive vital force which impels every natural species to maintain and preserve its own type; but it is raised to a far higher power by the deliberate effort of human knowledge and will to attain a known end. From these facts certain general conclusions follow. To begin with, education is not a practice which concerns the individual alone: it is essentially a function of the community. . . . The formative influence of the community on its members is most constantly active in its deliberate endeavour to educate each new generation of individuals so as to make them in its own image. The structure of every society is based on the written or unwritten laws which bind it and its members. Therefore, education in any human community (be it a family, a social class, a profession, or some wider complex such as a race or a state) is the direct expression of its active awareness of a *standard*. Now, education keeps pace with the life and growth of the community, and is altered both by changes imposed on it from without and by transformations in its internal structure and intellectual development. And, since the basis of education is a general consciousness of the values which govern human life, its history is affected by changes in the values current within the community.

Jaeger's use of the word "education" is far broader than that to which Americans are accustomed. *Paideia* is more than the sum of institutions: it is "the creation of a higher type of man. [The Greeks] believed that education embodied the purpose of all human effort. It was, they held, the ultimate justification for the existence of both the individual and the community." For Jaeger a description of the schools as a part of the way of life of any nation was not enough: he sought a concept of value, a consciously pursued ideal.

A discussion of American education from such a perspective would fill many volumes. This book has a narrower focus: to study American education as a reflection of the values of the community with reference particularly to the American ideal of equality of opportunity and the extent of its fulfillment in American schools, and to consider the nation's needs as they relate to the quality of its schools.

For American education must not only provide *an* education for everyone, but transmit the values of a democratic society and provide equal access for all to the best that education has to offer. Such a role for education as a force for the achievement of a democratic society has been given relatively little attention by American historians. There have been excellent accounts of particular colleges and universities. But by and large the role of the schools in economic and social change has received too little attention from scholars. Even the comments on education of those shrewd observers from abroad, de Tocqueville and Bryce, who so profoundly influenced the American's view of himself, have served to stimulate the speculations of only a few later observers of American education like Conant. Left to themselves, with little help or informed criticism from scholars, the specialists in educational matters have, until Cremin's and Hofstadter's recent works, had to build their own account of the history and the present standing of the schools and colleges. It is small wonder that these accounts are usually of interest only to those of like mind. The story of the triumph of the public school over its adversaries has been written as a chapter in the works of Horatio Alger, and Alger was read only by the generation which saw itself in his images. So the histories of education influenced those who saw themselves as a part of the struggles described, which usually meant the educators themselves. As a result, there is no common pattern of thought in the American mind about the role of the schools and colleges in national development. Yet, born in a Puritan age when man with a Bible had to fashion his life on earth and in heaven, education finds itself three centuries later the social agent for racial understanding. Both of these functions for the schools—individual salvation and social transformation—are still relevant in American thought. So are countless others, bred of change in family and social and economic life. Few if any Americans, however, carry the whole picture in mind, perhaps because no over-all pattern has been available to them—or perhaps because the tradition of decentralized management of the schools discourages the effort. Compare the relative clarity of the context into which the work of any contemporary politician, journalist, or writer is put—as the result of the writing on American history of Beard or Parrington or the two Schlesingers—with the absence of such comparative guideposts for the work of a contemporary educator. The very brilliance and individuality of *The Education of Henry Adams* makes it a poor model for an understanding of the schools and colleges of Adams' own or a later generation. No novel on education has painted a scene broad enough to catch the eye. Nor, with the possible exception of a few years in the early days of the republic, a few years in the era of reform before the Civil War, and now the mid-twentieth century, has the place of education risen to national attention through press or pamphlet. Can one wonder that the busy citizen sees only that part of his nation's system of education which happens to stand before him—his neighborhood school or his son's college scholarship? Or that he has but little interest in the sounds of occasional battles among the schools of educational thought that reach his ears? The citizen has been uninformed of the issues, often called on only when it is too late to do more than bind up the wounds and pay the costs. His patience has been sorely tried by a sequence of demands for local taxes or college tuition or alumni gifts. He has been encouraged by the educators themselves to think strictly in local terms because so many schools and colleges have for scores of years been locally financed. The citizen is hard put to keep his perspective.

The lot of the "professional" educator—as distinct from the scientist and scholar—is perhaps even more affected by the lack of perspective. Poor in public prestige and usually also in the goods of this world, he is further hurt by his isolation. The public sees only dimly what he is doing, and he is himself by no means certain of his position. The result has been the creation of a separate class of citizens, a kind of fifth estate, with an "identity" problem. Considered in a vague way to be useful, and sometimes suspected of being powerful, the educator is nevertheless not quite trusted in the affairs of the world. Increasingly he has built his own social life and professional protection. School and college teachers, who have only recently been joining forces after long years of estrangement from each other, are nevertheless both isolated from a public that fails to comprehend their relationship to the society as a whole.

Understanding education is all the more urgent for, in the old-fashioned American sense of the word "revolution," a necessary revolution is under way in American education today, and it will affect every citizen. Revolution has traditionally meant a transformation, a movement away from things as they were toward a new society. The philosophers of the original political revolutions talked eloquently of social transformation yet they seldom, if ever, mentioned education as an instrument of social change. The American Constitution itself does not even refer to education. Education was first a private matter, then a matter of concern to local communities. Until relatively recently, only a few federal programs concerned themselves with the schools. But today there is a national consciousness of the importance of education not only as an instrument for the fulfillment of the individual but also for the ultimate achievement of a democratic society, begun but by no means completed by the original American Revolution.

Revolution can be thought of in other ways as well—as a wheel turning in revolutions, moving as it turns. American education is on the move in this sense also but there is need to be certain that its movement is forward, the direction purposeful. Change is not automatically for the better. In education's history new fads and cults have often given the appearance of progress while failing to transform education for the good of the individual and for the good of society. It is imperative to review all programs for change with a critical eye for consequences, particularly in a time of revolution, when the pace of change discourages pause for reflection. We must be sure that the means—the techniques of change—serve the necessary goals of equality and of quality in education.

Yet the society is by no means clear about the goals it wishes education to serve. It is in conflict about its own basic values.

American society has immense faith in education. As Horace Mann said: "Education . . . beyond all other devices of human origin, is the great equalizer of the conditions of man—the balance-wheel of the social machinery. . . . It does better than to disarm the poor of their hostility towards the rich; it prevents being poor." American society expects a great deal from its schools and its expectations are based on a variety of assumptions about private and public responsibility, about individual and social needs. Yet these assumptions are often inconsistent even though they are often held by the same individual. Among the seemingly contradictory beliefs about education, which the majority of Americans appear to hold, are these:

1. That schooling is a good thing for everyone.
2. That by and large the more schooling the better.
3. That in a society that prides itself on mobility, schools are the avenue to the social betterment of the individual; that a child who does not learn will never amount to much.
4. That success, or doing a good job, in competition after the early childhood protective years—*whatever* the competition—is a

good thing; that education should be useful and practical to the individual, for society itself is competitive and the best time for the child to start the race and get used to the pace is now.

5. That the school is responsible for the encouragement of proper social and moral behavior, which includes unselfish habits.

6. That a certain degree of instruction is necessary to enable every citizen to make the sound decisions on public affairs needed in a democratic society.

7. That individuals and groups in a complex society of many races, religions, and social backgrounds should be taught to get along together by the schools.

8. That the schools must prepare youth to take on complex tasks in a complex society, and that selection of the better minds is needed by the society and is a function of the school.

More rarely will the further premise be presented that education means knowledge for its own sake, that the educated man is one who can come closer to an understanding of what is, after all, the really important subject in life: man's relation to God and His universe. Educators today speak little of such matters, yet the implied relation of man to divinity seems even now to influence the American attitude toward education. It cuts across other assumptions and sometimes conflicts with them. For our present purpose, however, it may be enough to record with a thoughtful pause that such an assumption surely would have been the first in education only a few decades ago.

The first four assumptions, at many points, appear to challenge the last four. American society remains competitive; yet it admires and often seeks the goals of a cooperative society in which the good of the whole may take precedence over the good of the individual, or at least may attempt reconciliation with it. Many of the failures of contemporary American education can be traced to this unresolved relationship. America had believed that it need only provide universal free education and all would be well. It did not realize that in a competitive society some schools would be more prosperous than others and some children would be neglected and deprived. Yet equality in a competitive society can only be provided by deliberate emphasis on cooperative effort to achieve the conditions under which competition is meaningful. American education has been oriented toward success; but it has failed to release the potential of many thousands of students. All children must be helped to be fit enough to survive if the success of the majority is not to become an exploitation of the rest.

Competitive assumptions appear in every discussion of the contemporary secondary school. Some critics say, for example, that the mind is insufficiently sharpened, that habits of hard work are not instilled, that the search for security rather than for success is fostered in the schools. There is far less parental concern about "cooperation" and "getting along with other types of children" than about removing their children from "bad" influences. The public school is less a "common" school for all classes of children than the ideals of democracy suggest. Contemporary social forces, such as zoning ordinances, wealthy suburbs, the concentration of urban ghettos, make mutual understanding between social classes of student in many ways more difficult than such understanding was fifty years ago. The success of some is made more certain but it is often achieved at the expense of others.

Families sensitive to social distinction (and it is the courageous observer who dares to discount the number) will tend to describe as "better" the school which is so placed that it draws more on the children of middle or upper class groups, in contrast to that which draws on the children of lower class groups. Frankness will sometimes reveal that behind such concern with quality lies racial and religious, as well as social class, discrimination. But parents claim that in such a school intellectual standards are higher, that the children are free from exposure to poor moral standards, and that they therefore will be less inclined toward antisocial behavior. It is true that intellectual attainments are likely to be higher in such selective schools. The subtleties of parental reward and punishment and the higher motivation of teachers tend to raise standards. Whether the moral standards are better is a matter of debate. A sense of justice is as much a moral standard as is the lack of delinquency.

It is assumed further that children from the "better" school will compete more successfully in the future for rewarding careers and social standing. Within the framework of a mobile society, in which social position is highly sensitive to the nature of employment and/or financial capacity, this is primarily a competitive notion and clearly it is in conflict with those aims for education which emphasize cooperation. Thus, withdrawal of middle or upper class children, regardless of race or religion, into "better" schools and communities tends to reduce the capacity of the community left behind.

Yet most parents, while respecting the rigors of competition, do not necessarily like its results. The Jacksonian tradition of equality is still strong within us; so, too, is the conviction that cooperation and mutual understanding are a good thing. The secondary school has, therefore, become an unwitting battlefield in the current conflict between those values in society as a whole which support competition and those which support cooperation. Many believe that there is an inherent contradiction between the goals of quality and of equality. They respect them both but when forced—or apparently forced—to make a personal choice between them, they choose the goals of quality, knowing that quality is necessary for success in a competitive society. The goals of cooperation suffer in consequence.

So, too, society has given the *lowest* status among educators to those teachers who are expected to create desirable cooperative attitudes in the children under their tutelage—that is, the teachers in elementary school, who are expected to see to it that the children love one another, who are expected to play no favorites in rewarding the intellectually promising above others, and who are directed to conform in their personal behavior to the strictest moral standards of the community. The *highest* esteem, on the other hand, is granted to the teacher at the other end of the academic procession—the renowned university professor who is expected to function as a competitive mentor, perhaps distant from his students, often more feared than loved; the judge of success, the rewarder of progress. He himself is expected to succeed in academic competition, a race which varies with the institution but which usually involves measures of scholarly competence and reputation. These too are high standards, but competitive in character, of a very different type from the standards of cooperation used to judge the teacher of younger children.

The schizophrenic state of the high school teacher, placed between these two extremes of cooperation and competition, is reflected in the public ambivalence about his role. If he is really good at his subject, it is asked, why is he not a college teacher? If he wants to weld social groups into happy partnership, why does he not spend his time in the elementary school, or go into social work, or do something more effective toward his goal? Yet woe betide him if he takes too seriously his role as both prosecutor and judge of intellectual standards, and insists on rigid competition or more work than the intellectual, social, or athletic mood of the community will permit. It may be that in the mid-twentieth century in the United States scientific competition with other nations and renewed dedication to education in a Great Society may cause a change in this mood, with more social approval granted to intellectual success alone. But today the high school teacher has neither the freedom of the college professor nor the relative clarity of function of the elementary teacher. Under such circumstances it is scarcely astonishing that many high school teachers tend to identify themselves with the subject they teach (as biologists or historians rather than educators), believing that this characteristic of their collegiate colleagues (who always think of themselves in these terms) is the reason for their higher standing in the public eye. Nor should it be a surprise that others seek administrative positions, not only for the higher salaries involved, but also in search of a more clearly defined social role. For the man who has to be prosecutor, counsel for the defense, and judge at the same time, the conflict between competition and cooperation is hard to bear.

The contest between these assumptions in the public mind lies at the very heart of the tasks facing all those concerned with educational policy. It crosses all barriers between sect and class. It can rarely be traced to differences in views between various groups in society. It is not sensible to conclude that one economic group believes in certain of these assumptions but not in others, or that a particular political or religious group differs in these assumptions in a predictable way from another. The dilemma confronts them all.

The history of the United States itself can be expressed as a conflict between the concepts of a competitive society and the ideals of a harmonious cooperative community. The sociologist may see the signs of hardening in the social arteries—a sharpening of racial or social class differences—while his colleague in the humanities may decry less stringent scholarly standards as a prelude to a lowering, or a leveling, to a depressing, middle class plateau. The conflict of assumptions rests not alone within groups: it rests within each American citizen. Do the values of the American community suggest a permanent schizophrenia between the goals of competition and cooperation? between quality and equality? This book suggests, indeed affirms, that the schizophrenia must be cured, the conflict resolved, if the good of the society itself is not to be undermined. A clearer perspective on the issues is the best hope of either workable compromise or a higher synthesis and a greater logic.

Americans assume that the more formal education a child has the better. Yet education per se is no guarantee of a just society. The observer of the mid-twentieth century cannot forget that in his lifetime at least four governments with quite different beliefs from those of the United States have exploited the concept of more and more formal education for antidemocratic ends: fascism, Japanese imperialism, Russian and Chinese communism. The observer may therefore ask whether the implications of the educator's doctrine of extensive education for its own sake have been adequately explored. What might be the result, to use an example brought to mind by Germany's Weimar Republic, of the rise in the number of discontented intellectuals? Might they not, as many did in Germany in the thirties, provide the intellectual setting for an authoritarian movement? To this concern it is significant that the American historian might reply: Not as long as the intellectuals are kept in close touch with the mass of the people, not as long as the American pattern permits social relationships in youth between the worker with his hands and the white-collar employee, not as long as racial or class lines are not identified with a particular kind of education. If the society creates rigid barriers, and removes the means of flexibility and mobility, the sociologist might say, it runs the risk of the disillusion which was in part (not, of course, alone) responsible for the rise of the Nazi movement.

The ideals of cooperation, therefore, may be seen as more than ideals, as the practical, indeed essential, foundation of a durable democracy. The energies generated in the tensions between cooperation and competition sustain democracy; yet they can hardly be assigned equal merit, for without a certain basis of cooperation, the very conditions which promote competition will themselves disappear. If cooperative ideals are to be reconciled with competitive goals, American education requires a continuing transformation.

American education rests on two assumptions from which all else derives: the idea that man is potentially good and that this good can be brought about by education. Americans have a sense of pride in the immensity of the national endeavor to educate all the people. Partly this is the pride of the strong nation convinced that its way of life is better than anyone else's. But behind this pride is a hope—or, perhaps better, a belief. It is belief in the idea of progress. To assume that the more schooling the child has, the better, is to say that man can always learn, that he has the possibility of perfection within him. The concept of education for all children is based on the same optimistic estimate of the nature of the human being. Despite all the discouragements and the daily disappointments of the teacher, despite the stubborn facts of behavior in many children, despite the evidence of vast differences in abilities, the American educational system renews each day its faith in this principle of the perfectibility of man. In the doctrine of the perfectibility of man, the goals of quality and equality in the necessary revolution in American education are joined. For perfectibility implies the ability of all to learn, and the duty of society to teach. The contemporary task is to make this doctrine real in the lives of all of our children.

The roots of this idea, of course, lie deep in the religious and political inheritance of the people. Even in the gloomiest days of the doctrine of predestination, it was thought worthwhile to teach the children enough to be able to read the Scriptures, so that they might try to govern their lives by its standards. With the advent of more hopeful doctrines came a surging wave of optimism about the chances of man to better not only himself but the whole of society. The stories of the Utopian groups of the nineteenth century are a familiar part of our tradition. So is the story of frontier American's confidence in his ability to govern himself and to create a better society. Man could learn; man was able to trust himself.

In the American West this confidence in self, however, was not based on learning as the word is often used today—that is, learning from books. The intellectual may have been a favorite in New England in the first part of the nineteenth century, but he was no hero west of the Appalachians. To the frontiersman, there was a link between a certain kind of book learning and the aristocrat—and it was from the aristocrat that he removed himself when he left for the West. Yet the notion of man's perfectibility did not depend on formal teaching; it depended rather on an attitude of mind, what Whitehead described as a climate of thought. The fact that it may have had its roots in a long tradition of Christian thinking on the one hand, or in the ideas of Rousseau on the other, was of little importance. The present realities were more important. It did not take a book to see that man could remake nature, that he could establish his own society. There it was before the eye for anyone to see. Man went to the school of nature and of experience. The school as we know it was useful for learning certain elementary skills of reading and writing and ciphering, but the main task lay ahead in adult life. This is the tradition that still affects many an intellectual who seeks the votes of his countrymen for political office. Yet in the West, more than in the East, the public school was the common school. In the older Eastern cities, the first public schools were often the pauper schools, the children of the "respectable" class went to private schools. In the West everyone's children attended the public schools. The notion of equality was characteristic of the frontier.

Such was the doctrine of perfectibility as it was interpreted in earlier days in the West. But as the nation became more industrialized, the task of learning became less simple. To advance in life required more than the simple skills. The movement for free public education was one of the first causes assumed by the early labor movements a century ago. In a more complex society dependent on trained intelligence, the achievement of the perfectibility of man required more formal schooling. Thoreau may have returned to nature after Harvard College, but he was an exception.

In the optimistic interpretation of the nature of man the idea of the capacity to learn was linked to the larger idea of progress. Things were going to get better if man would only do something about it. The doctrine of evil in man, the notion that pessimism was the only wise policy in human affairs, was not popular in the early nineteenth century, and despite two global wars and the contrary convictions of certain philosophers and theologians, it is not popular in America more than a century later.

Basic optimism is a bond between the varied philosophies and institutional arrangements of American education. The educational patterns we inherit today were established by such optimists as Franklin and Jefferson, Mann and Barnard, Dewey and the social reformers of the early twentieth century. The ideas behind public schools are in the Jacksonian, not in the more conservative Hamiltonian traditions. Those most influential in setting their tone were men who lived in the heady age of social reform, whether in the early days of the Massachusetts Bay Colony, or in the New England of Channing and Emerson, or in America of the New Deal and the Great Society. The public schools and the public colleges and universities have sustained their dreams in years of hope and optimism about the place of man on earth; they have lost their vitality or at best have sought to consolidate gains in years of cynicism and pessimism.

The educator who has his doubts about the perfectibility of all men is restless and ill at ease in a school designed for all children. He can see in the imperfections of the child before him the imperfections of the man to come. He may doubt whether there can be progress in society if the child cannot grow into responsibility with a capacity for wise judgment. He will be happier when a prior selection has been made, when optimism about all children is tempered by the selection of a few. He will, in short, be more content when the policies by which the school is managed seem in closer alignment with brute fact. The educator in a democratic society, therefore, must come to accept the doctrine of perfectibility (perhaps without conscious thought) or must seek some other way of earning his bread if he is to escape constant conflict.

The great majority of educators are probably in the tradition of the founders of the public schools, despite continual frustration and discouragement at the obstinate resistance of their pupils to the process of learning. Yet the constant exhortations of their leaders in the National Education Association on the need of education for all seems to testify that the cup of hope needs refilling at regular intervals. The American people assign to the schools the task of putting the hope of perfectibility into practice—but they spend their own time worrying about other, more "practical" matters. The teacher is supposed to put into practice on weekdays what many Americans hear only in their churches on Sundays, and American schools are expected to transmit the publicly espoused values of the community even when the community itself often rejects them in practice.

This bond which unites the educators and accounts in part for the similarity of most American schools despite differences in size and quality, at the same time isolates the educator. The majority of occupations in a complex society are not based on any such assumption of human perfectibility. Many, indeed, are based on quite opposite assumptions. The teacher's work stands in a genuine sense as the living criticism of the parts of the society which he serves. The natural links with the ministry, which he enjoyed in the first two centuries of American history, are now largely broken; yet his is a kind of secular ministry. Isolated from the "real society," teachers are often a lonely crowd seeking encouragement and inspiration. And loneliness may bring disillusion, and with disillusion may come division and doubt about the values of education itself.

Education for all, they may come to suspect, may become education for none, a conclusion which strikes at the root not only of the idea of perfectibility, but also of the idea of equality that is so firmly imbedded in the political history of the United States. Some of the disputes about education policy have reflected more the loss of hope than the loss of conviction. The American teacher can understandably sometimes be tempted to surrender to doubts as he faces the material before him, but he cannot in practice yield to them without conflict with the purpose of the schools. The fact that much of public education reflects divisions of class and race, the separation of children by too rigid testing into different "tracks," the neglect of the schools that need quality the most, are all evidence of an erosion of the American self-image and of the schism between the ideal and the reality. The schools cannot accept such practices without subverting their own purposes.

Educators tend to falter when they have reason to doubt that their optimistic assumption about the nature of man and their hope for success in carrying out its implications are shared by the majority. If there is public cynicism about their motives their defense crumbles.

Some of the stories of the schools in the Depression illustrate this point. So do deprived school systems in economically depressed areas where teachers may doubt the most basic premise of education—the capacity of the child to learn. Even in a period of general prosperity one observes that the teachers and administrators from such areas are not active in their professional associations. They tend to lose contact with the colleges in which they received their training. They tend to be out of touch with the latest ideas and with the best modern teaching materials. They are, in short, isolated. As a result they become especially vulnerable to local attack. It is in such circumstances that the pattern of local control gives the worst account of itself. If such areas should grow in number, and if the general climate of optimism about the potential accomplishments of education should change to one of doubt and pessimism, then the bonds that now tie the schools together may be expected to weaken, and the cherished democratic ideal of education will be undermined. Schools for the majority, based on a concept of human perfectibility, are less than honest if, by implication, they exclude members of certain races and classes from that concept. No school lives in

Table 1. Percent of illiteracy[1] in the population: United States, 1900 to 1960

Year	Per cent illiterate[2]
1900	11.3
1910	8.3
1920	6.5
1930	4.8
1950[3]	3.3
1960[3]	2.4

1 Illiteracy is defined as the inability to read and write a simple message either in English or in any other language.

2 Percentages refer to the population 15 years old and over from 1900 to 1930, and to the population 14 years old and over in 1950 and 1960.

3 Estimated.

Note: Data are for 50 States and the District of Columbia.

SOURCE: U.S. Department of Commerce, Bureau of the Census, *Current Population Reports*, Series P-23, No. 8.

isolation, and any appearance to the contrary is an illusion. The neglect of the deprived school effectively corrodes the education of the privileged.

The balance is a delicate one. Enthusiasm without realism has formed some strange educational policy. Realism without optimism would end with no education at all.

II   The First and the Second Revolutions

It has been the American assumption—and the subject of many a Fourth of July oration since Jefferson put the idea into eloquent and persuasive words—that democracy is impossible without education. The public schools were established to spread literacy and general knowledge throughout the population, making possible an informed electorate that could be achieved no other way.

In the wake of the waves of immigration in the nineteenth and twentieth centuries, the number of students in American secondary schools doubled between 1910 and 1920 and increased more than twentyfold between 1900 and the present. A revolution of American education was under way, stimulated by labor unions, reform groups, and others, a revolution that stirred the melting pot and "Americanized," to use the word popular at the time, millions of new citizens.

The spread of education through all the social levels and classes in the United States is one of the nation's remarkable achievements. Each hamlet put it into effect. It was done by and large by local initiative and by some state encouragement, not by the federal government. No other country did it though some other countries were just as rich as we. The British could have done it; they did not. By the beginning of the Second World War, this revolution in education was substantially accomplished. It was a daring idea providing access to educational opportunity for all children. Its principal concern was to train citizens for a democracy; it showed less anxiety about quality. Quality and equality are to constitute the coming revolution in American education.

The record of that first revolution in American education is worth study. Young adults twenty-five to twenty-nine years of age have completed, on the average, about twelve and a half years of schooling (according to a Bureau of the Census report containing data for

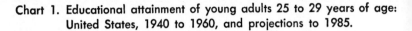

Chart 1. Educational attainment of young adults 25 to 29 years of age: United States, 1940 to 1960, and projections to 1985.

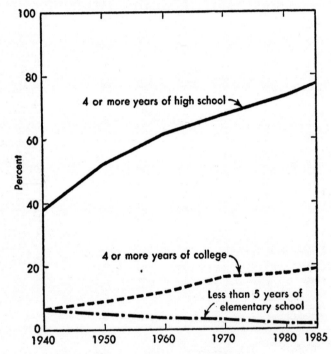

SOURCE: U.S. Department of Commerce, Bureau of the Census.

March 1964), compared with a median educational attainment of approximately eight and a half years for the population sixty-five years of age and over. Thus, in little more than a generation, the education of the average individual in this country has been lengthened by four full years. More than 69 percent of the young adults are high school graduates, and nearly 13 percent of them have completed four or more years of college, while among the population sixty-five years of age and over, only 22 percent are high school graduates, and fewer than 5 percent have finished college.

The necessary revolution in education today finds many relentless forces bearing upon it that challenge the newer goals of quality

Chart 2. The enrollment explosion

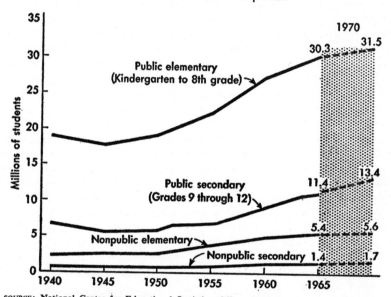

SOURCE: National Center for Educational Statistics, Office of Education of the U.S. Department of Health, Education, and Welfare: Digest of Educational Statistics, 1965; Projections of Educational Statistics to 1974–75.

and of equality. Despite generally lower birth rates, America is rearing increasing numbers of school-age children because there are more and more women of childbearing age. Based upon population projections by the Bureau of the Census, elementary and secondary school enrollment is expected to climb from 48.4 million in 1964 to 54.9 million in 1974 to 66 million in 1984—an increase of 36 percent over the 1964 figure and 20 percent over the 1974 figure. Nearly one million students a year will be added to the enrollments of the nation's schools. The goal of education for all children has been in large measure successful. It has been a major factor in the "melting pot."

The process has not been without its critics. Many Americans not only believe that it is time to drop the melting-pot approach, but also are inclined to think that the schools and the mass media have carried the process too far in the first place. Some of the advocates of cultural

Table 2. Number of high school graduates compared with population 17 years of age: United States, selected years from 1869–70 to 1963–64

| School year | Population 17 years old[2] | High school graduates[1] | | | Number graduated per 100 persons 17 years of age |
		Total	Boys	Girls	
1869–70	815,000	16,000	7,064	8,936	2.0
1879–80	946,026	23,634	10,605	13,029	2.5
1889–90	1,259,177	43,731	18,549	25,182	3.5
1899–1900	1,489,146	94,883	38,075	56,808	6.4
1909–10	1,786,240	156,429	63,676	92,753	8.8
1919–20	1,855,173	311,266	123,684	187,582	16.8
1929–30	2,295,822	666,904	300,376	366,528	29.0
1939–40	2,403,074	1,221,475	578,718	642,757	50.8
1949–50	2,034,450	1,199,700	570,700	629,000	59.0
1951–52	2,040,800	1,196,500	569,200	627,300	58.6
1953–54	2,128,600	1,276,100	612,500	663,600	60.0
1955–56	2,270,000	1,414,800	679,500	735,300	62.3
1957–58	2,324,000	1,505,900	725,500	780,400	64.8
1959–60	2,862,005	1,864,000	898,000	966,000	65.1
1961–62	2,768,000	1,925,000	941,000	984,000	69.5
1963–64	3,001,000	2,290,000	1,121,000	1,169,000	76.3

1 Includes graduates of public and nonpublic schools.

2 Data from the Bureau of the Census.

Note: Beginning in 1959–60, includes Alaska and Hawaii.

SOURCE: U.S. Department of Health, Education, and Welfare, Office of Education, *Digest of Educational Statistics.*

pluralism argue that there is a danger of too much conformity. The argument is that once the minimum needs for social unity have been met (and for immigrant groups in general, they were met some years ago), individual and group differences should be permitted to enrich society.

Not all minority groups, however, have moved into full acceptance in American society. Some are still on their way. During the last twenty-five years, for example, much progress has been made in accepting Americans of Asian origin. Except in some communities on the Pacific coast where local prejudice has a long history, Asian-Americans are usually able to find jobs, to secure admission to schools, and to live where they choose. This quiet transition from a status once regarded as unassimilable has attracted little public attention, but it is real nonetheless. Yet it is still not complete.

The Spanish-speaking peoples—Puerto Ricans (mostly in New York City) and the Mexicans in the American Southwest (more than three million people altogether but with a figure of six million predicted through immigration and natural increase)—have not yet been assimilated either to their own satisfaction or to the satisfaction of American society at large. The problems of these two groups do not seem to be vastly different from those faced by the Germans of the 1840's or the Polish of the early 1900's. They, too, did not know the English language, they understood little of the privileges and duties of citizenship, they were unfamiliar with the history of the United States, they lacked the habits and social skills necessary for full participation in American society. Yet, eventually, we may expect that the Mexicans and Puerto Ricans, like the Germans and Poles, will move from the ghettos to mixed neighborhoods, and then to "all-American" neighborhoods where they will merge as separate nationality groups into the larger whole.

The assimilation of America's 550,000 Indians is less successful. About 170,000 have left the reservations to live among the general population and have sent their children to local public schools. About one-third of the children from the 380,000 majority attend Indian schools in isolated areas, such as the vast reaches of the 24,000-square-mile Navajo reservation in Arizona, New Mexico, and Utah.

Many others attend small inadequately supported public schools. The deficiencies of these schools were demonstrated through World War II Selective Service tests, which disqualified most Indians for service in the armed forces because of lack of educational attainment. Since the war, the U. S. Bureau of Indian Affairs and other private and public organizations have tried to convert these schools from poor-quality manual-training institutions to good technical and, in some cases, college-preparatory schools. Yet in 1960, only 18.5 percent of the Indian population twenty-five years of age and over had finished high school.

The greatest failure of the melting pot, however, is the American Negro. It is, as Myrdal put it, the American Dilemma. American society, partly through the schools, has been able to assimilate millions of immigrants from Europe, from Latin America, and from Asia into an American culture and has granted them full citizenship. It has not been able to assimilate the American Negro. Even those immigrants who arrived in recent decades have gained a membership in American society denied to the descendants of Negroes who were brought to America before 1800.

One may ask why the schools in our great cities, so successful in assimilating children of immigrants into the national culture, have apparently failed to perform the same service for Negro children. The racist explains the failure by alleging racial or social inferiority. Some historians say the immigrant brought his own culture and sense of nationality with him, but others point out that many immigrants, poor and dispossessed, had little culture to bring, and many peasants arrived in American cities as uneducated, as unorganized, and as poorly equipped for urban living as many Negroes arriving from the South today. But they did not, as the Negroes did, arrive in America as slaves; their families were not broken up; their women were not exploited; they were not despised as somehow less than human. And that difference is basic—one not of degree but of kind. American society—and its schools and colleges are a direct reflection of that society—has not yet overcome its tragic heritage of slavery. School segregation and the educational deficiencies of the mass of American Negroes today are a direct legacy of that heritage.

Also excluded from many benefits of education are the American poor, both white and Negro. For although the goal of universal secondary education is now more than two-thirds reached, education beyond the high school remains to a considerable extent selective. The public hears about the six out of ten high school graduates who go on to some form of post high school education. The public until recently heard less about the waste of our human resources—the three out of ten American young people who fail to complete high school at all, the 5 percent who do not even complete the eighth grade. Few among the general public realize that the upper three-fourths of the graduates of certain high schools are better prepared for college than the upper tenth in many other schools. Studies in 1962 by Project Talent, financed by the Office of Education, showed that almost one-quarter (23 percent) of high school seniors in the 80–90 academic percentile of their class and about one-third (34 percent) of those in the 70–80 percentile failed to enter college.

Data from Project Talent show that about 15 percent of the most capable high school graduates with IQ's of 120 and above do not continue their education and most are unable to do so because of financial need. Project Talent demonstrated that youths from low income families, regardless of academic ability, have a far poorer chance of going to college than their classmates from upper income families. The students in the top 2 percent of their class who reach college regardless of family income get there because numerous colleges are on the lookout for such exceptional candidates, but below this top level, the facts are far less encouraging. Of American high school boys in the second quarter in academic aptitude, 51.8 percent from families with incomes below $3,000 per year fail to enter college, as contrasted with only 20.3 percent from families with incomes above $12,000. For girls the situation is even more inequitable; in the second quarter in general college aptitude, 74.8 percent of students from families with incomes below $3,000 annually fail to enter college compared with 29.2 percent from families with incomes over $12,000.

In the school year 1962–63, the average direct cost of attending college was approximately $1,480 in public institutions, with a $2,400 average predicted by 1980. During the next twenty-five years, disposable family income is expected to increase by about 32 percent while some estimates of college charges predict an increase about 75 percent. When these costs are compared with the annual median family income of $6,600 in 1964, it is evident how substantial an outlay college education now represents for American families. As a major item of family expenditure, it is exceeded only by the cost of a home. That opportunities for higher education are dependent upon the family's ability to pay is further shown by the fact that private

Table 3. Estimated costs for attending college

Year	Public	Private
1980–81	$2,400	$3,640
1976–77	2,160	3,280
1970–71	1,840	2,780
1964–65	1,560	2,370
1958–59	1,330	1,950
1954–55	1,190	1,700
1948–49	1,010	1,380
1942–43	860	1,120
1936–37	790	1,020
1930–31	730	960

SOURCE: Office of Education of U.S. Department of Health, Education, and Welfare.

higher educational institutions continue to draw about one-half and the public institutions about one-quarter of their students from the top 10 percent of the nation's income level.

It may be said that the nation as a whole did not fully accept the idea of public responsibility for universal educational opportunity beyond the high school for those of ability and interest until the mid-1960's. Today, to propose a universal two years beyond high school is not a radical concept, but rather seems an expansion of the historical concept of universal secondary education. This new commitment, of course, does not suggest that everyone needs the same kind of higher education. Selectivity will obviously be maintained in professional and technological education as well as in some private colleges, but the phenomenal expansion of community and junior colleges shows the trend. There are those who argue that provision of higher education for an ever-larger segment of American youth will be, if not a catastrophe, at least the spawning of mediocrity. Others, now the majority, claim that higher education can challenge the brilliant and serve the not-so-brilliant at the same time. On one point there can be little debate: a complex democratic, industrialized society cannot advance and expand through the efforts of an elite alone, even if the few are selected on the basis of aptitude rather than privilege. The preservation and enrichment of society rest on the services of citizens with both modest and exceptional abilities. The Educational Policies Commission pointed out that the important question in the future is not, Who deserves to be educated? but rather, Whom can society, in conscience and self-interest, exclude?"

A civilized society turns upon the strength of its educational axis. Ninety-nine percent of American children aged six to thirteen attend school. Approximately 93 percent of those children of high school age (i.e., from fourteen to seventeen) attend school, and more than 70 percent of our young people now graduate, though there is wide variation from state to state and within states. Of these high school graduates, slightly more than one-half enrolled in colleges and universities. This proportion is rising. Yet, as we have seen, we cannot claim that we have achieved equal educational opportunity, even under a system proud of its record of offering twelve years of free public schooling. Approximately 19.5 million Americans eighteen years of age or older have completed fewer than eight years of schooling. Among them are about eight million functional illiterates with fewer than five years of schooling. In eight of the states, the adult population in 1960 had a median education of less than nine years. Even in the top seven states nearly half of the adults had less than a high school education.

Equality of educational opportunity throughout the nation continues today for many to be more a myth than a reality. The rise in school and college enrollment has not kept pace with society's needs for an educated citizenry.

Within the last decade, the number of jobs specifying four or more years of college increased by 54 percent. In the decade of 1950–60, the number of employed technical and professional workers increased by 66 percent, while employment for unskilled industrial workers increased by only 4 percent, and farm laborers decreased by 13 percent. Four percent of the labor force was unemployed at the end of 1965, and among American youth from sixteen to nineteen years of age who are out of school, the unemployment rate was four times the adult rate in 1965. The unemployment rate of nonwhites is dramatically higher: 7 percent are unemployed today and 25 percent of nonwhites from sixteen to nineteen years of age are out of work. Automation and other technical advances have displaced many unskilled jobs. The coming years could lead to both soaring industrial productivity and—some fear—to a yawning gap of unemployment and unfulfillment. The demand for more trained professional and technical people will accelerate. Employment opportunities for the untrained, the unskilled, the undereducated worker may continue to decline. Education, the institution that can do the most to prevent the accumulation of an unskilled labor force, has not met its responsibility.

A necessary revolution in American education implies continuing education. No longer can individuals talk of "completing" their education. For those who move to college and graduate school and into the professions there is constant need to keep up to date. In the field of medicine, to take one dramatic example, advances in research save lives, and no physician can afford to let his learning end with medical school. So, too, in business and industry, faced by the technological progress of automation, workers need frequent retraining if their skills are not to become obsolescent and if they themselves are not to become unemployable. With the trend toward earlier retirement and longevity, there is need also for adult education to bring new dimensions of meaning to the lives of older persons. The day when the community could afford a "fortress" school, dark and locked at night and on weekends, has gone. Future schools and colleges must become truly community education and cultural centers.

As economists developed better instruments for measuring, some were convinced that they could not account for the rate of growth of the national product only by investment in hardware (machinery) or in labor. The missing factors were investment in research and development and education of the working force. Education, one of the primary ways to achieve both quality performance and equality of opportunity, is now understood also as a necessary national investment for an expanding society. It is not only a commodity to be consumed by the individual but an investment whose use brings returns both to the individual and to the society. As with America's participation in the growth of underdeveloped countries in Point 4, ICA, and AID, the emphasis in education at home is on investment for the future. The new "missionary" abroad is the economist, interested in the development of resources. So also it is the economist who points to the need for education in American society. It is not that national self-interest alone justifies education—education is of value for its own sake and enriches the lives of individuals—but rather that it has become increasingly apparent that equal educational opportunity is necessary to the maintenance of a free and a prosperous society. In education, the human being benefits and so does the nation. The idealistic and the practical and the private and public goals are one.

Other countries have often chosen to educate their upper class and their lower class in separate streams. America has historically chosen the opposite way, believing that democracy draws its strength from a society where class lines are blurred rather than sharpened. Indeed, the public schools effectively helped to bring generations of children of immigrants and others into the American middle class culture. With more education, income rose, consumption increased. Yet this historic American boast is now increasingly endangered. In urban ghettos, education without quality has reinforced a lower class status among Negroes and the children of the poor, while in comfortable suburbs education of quality has enhanced an upper-middle class elite.

Other countries are moving toward the traditional American goal of compulsory and comprehensive education for all. England, for example, where the members of the lower classes have not previously gone beyond the fifteenth year of school unless they were unusually talented, has recently embarked on a program of equal education for students who earlier were bypassed. How ironic it would be to find that America has persuaded others of the practicality of its dream only to lose it at home!

The United States has protected the right of parents to send their children to private or parochial schools rather than to public schools. And in a mobile society, parents may pick up stakes and move to another community if the schools do not suit them where they are. Many white middle class American families are moving to suburbs to escape urban schools. Though we would not consider interfering with the basic freedom to move, many persons in America do not have the luxury of such choice; they are restricted to certain areas either because they are poor or because they are Negro, or both. Yet we believe that they, too, have rights. Their children have a right not to be separated from others involuntarily, either by economic or racial barriers. A caste society violates the style of American democracy.

And beyond the rights of individuals to separate voluntarily but not to be separated involuntarily—two seemingly (but surely not) conflicting rights—lies the right of a democratic society-as-a-whole. Society has the inevitable duty to educate its citizens to live according to its way—in the case of America, to live in democracy. It has insisted on compulsory education. It may well be that learning to read is no more important to a child than learning how to get along with children who are brighter or less bright than himself, who are richer or poorer than he, who come from a race or religion or national background different from his own. Adult society is not protected from such difference. A child who lives in a hothouse may flounder as an adult when he finds around him in his business, his church, his street, persons he never met as a child. If the Negro child needs an integrated school to put the lie to his self-image of inferiority and to win the same quality of education available to white children, then the white child needs to avoid the elitist image of himself as superior. In the same way one could say that the right of a child to attend a parochial school—the right of free religious choice—may seem to conflict with the need of society to educate its future citizens in the habits of tolerance, learned most easily in daily face-to-face encounters with persons whose beliefs and backgrounds are different.

It depends, of course, on who goes to school, and how the school is managed. If the suburban public schools or the urban private schools become the refuge of the upper middle class, if the urban parochial schools become the refuge of the urban Catholic, and if the public schools of our largest cities become predominantly Negro and poor (as the current trend in cities like New York, Philadelphia, Boston, Chicago, and Washington would indicate) it is not alone the poor and the Negro who suffer deprivation, but the rich and the white as well.

Education has historically been a prime factor in making possible the upward social and economic mobility of the individual American. The American concept of equal opportunity is a liberating force in the development of the human mind. The individual who will contribute to and cope with the great social changes in the present and the future must be able to establish the conditions of his own dignity, and to recognize the dignity of others.

It is not an easy thing to educate in a democracy. Plato and Jefferson and Dewey sought solutions for their times, but every day makes the task harder. No longer can we think of universal literacy and a rudimentary knowledge of American history as the only requisites of citizenship. Economists now tell us that it is essential to democracy that its members develop to the fullest limit of their talents, whatever those talents may be, that they learn to be productive to society— whether they produce buildings, services, of poems—and that they learn how to live in a free society. Such demands pose what seem to be paradoxes of public policy. For example:

We believe in a pluralistic society of diverse groups existing together without turmoil, yet we may end with some form of self-imposed segregation. Are we in danger of conformity and mediocrity in a unified, integrated system of education? Should all students be treated equally or are some "more equal" than others? Is our commitment to individual freedom threatened by our concern for justice? Is our concern for justice threatened by our commitment to individual freedom? The society poses apparently unanswered questions but surely the answers are apparent in the American ideal. All students *must* have equality of opportunity. Such equality does *not* lead inevitably to mediocrity—indeed, quality itself is dependent on equality. Freedom and justice are *not* contradictory but essential to each other.

We have fallen too easily into a trap that seems to force us to choose between alternatives, as though we could not have quality education and equality at the same time, as though the comfortable would suffer if the poor were properly taught. For not only is the paradox misleading, but the exact opposite holds. We cannot have quality education without equality, nor are the comfortable safe if the poor do not learn. No isolation is possible in this interwoven, interrelated society where each man's vote affects the other and one man's discontent can set off a chain reaction that leaves no one untouched. American education can no longer afford the luxury of the contradiction in practice between quality of education and equality of educational opportunity. The solution of this contradiction is the second, and necessary, revolution.

III Inequality Based on Race and Class

In the last decade, the American majority has come to recognize that schools segregated by local law or custom, or by real estate covenants, are insupportable in modern society. This is not just because segregation is unfair or unjust or contrary to the Constitution, but because it results in bad education. A youngster's preparation to lead a significant, purposeful adult life requires the recognition that all classes and all races are important elements in American society. A system of education which fails to take account of that fundamental fact is as uneconomic as it is unfair. The following statement from a report made in June of 1965 by the Educational Policies Commission of the National Education Association and the American Association of School Administrators suggests the new tone of the 1960's, which followed decades of silence.

Segregation on grounds of race is bad. In education, it denies children, white or Negro, a chance to obtain a broader perspective on the society. It complicates the overcoming of racial stereotypes. In middle class schools, it breeds a sense of innate superiority which is unjustified and unhealthy. . . . The best way to build good relations between races is to enable each race to have experiences with the other which are welcome and fruitful and in which each race can come to see the other as composed of individuals and not stereotypes.

Under Title VI of the Civil Rights Act of 1964, the Office of Education is required to see to it that federal funds are not spent in schools and colleges that discriminate. The government intends to enforce that requirement and has been seeking ways to do so. Confronting it are the long-established customs of communities in both North and South where segregated education in fact survives. It is never easy to bring about basic changes in society, particularly when the national interest and consensus may conflict with the interests of the local majority as that majority perceives it. The problem does not afflict the South alone. The evidence suggests that *de facto* segregation in Northern cities is as difficult to dislodge as *de jure* segregation in the South.

For many years the Supreme Court ruled in effect that local communities could separate the Negro and the white students if they wished, provided that equal facilities were provided. The tendency of these "separate but equal" decisions was to reinforce the pattern of local and state control of separate but *unequal* education. The decision of the Supreme Court of 1954, requiring desegregation of schools, clearly affirms that the principle of federal policy must govern, whatever the wishes of the locality. The Civil Rights Act of 1964 added the power of the executive branch of the government. No one can deny that for a substantial, though declining, number of American citizens this decision represents a federal act which is contrary to their wishes. The national interest has, however, been deemed transcendent.

The federal government—judicial, executive, legislative—is now firmly committed to racial desegregation of the schools. After the Supreme Court decision of 1954, desegregation, in the sense of the opening of schools to persons of all races without discrimination, became the national policy. But the pace of change is slow, almost imperceptible in some areas, and—particularly in Northern urban areas —even retrogressive.

In cities throughout the North and South, "resegregation" is now taking place as white middle class families withdraw their children from the public schools or move into neighborhoods where schools remain white because the community is white. The record of the schools in the past decade is not as encouraging in practice as are the policies of the three branches of the federal government. The necessary revolution has a long distance to go.

The first year and a half of applying the antidiscrimination provisions of Title VI to the schools satisfied none of the parties involved. Only a small percentage of Negro students enrolled in formerly white schools in the South under the "free choice" plans permitted by federal guidelines. More than 95 percent of the Southern school boards submitted plans that were acceptable to the U.S. Office of Education for the fall of 1965, but there were serious difficulties with school districts that complained that they were being required to change long-established patterns too fast, and there were also grave charges—often justified—that plans were on paper only and that enforcement provisions were inadequate.

In the North, particularly in the large cities, *de facto* segregation aroused civil rights groups and led to tests of the application of the Civil Rights Act under circumstances in which the intent of Congress and the actions of the Executive branch were differently interpreted by officials and groups at local, state, and national levels. The values of the American community were undergoing a radical change, and, as Jaeger put it, "since the basis of education is a general consciousness of the values which govern human life, its history is affected by changes in the values current within the community." National policy, to which the overwhelming majority of the people agreed, was being put to the test in the reality of the social and economic life of the American community, and affected both the home and the school. The federal government in handling its part of the task had to see to it that its funds would not entrench *de facto* segregation, but rather facilitate desegregation. It was easy to predict that there would be trouble when deeply ingrained social values and interests were affected.

But there can be no question of the final outcome. Debate is over timing and method, not direction. Discrimination on the basis of race in American education must go. Children of different races must be educated together. Positive, not negative, action is needed. Leaders in all walks of life, and at all levels of government, will have to join hands, for the task is beyond the capacity of any one group, including the federal government and including the educators. Yet it is up to the educators, who above all must be sensitive to the underlying values of the society, to take the lead. And it is up to government to support them. No doubt some will be injured in the process, but such is the price of leadership. The conscience of the nation has spoken.

The problems of the future are going to be even more complex in many areas than those of the past.

In Washington, D.C., in 1953, 43.2 percent of the public school students were white and 56.8 percent Negro. In 1964, ten years after the Supreme Court desegregation decision of 1954, Negroes were 87.6 percent of the school population, and whites ("all others") had declined to 12.4 percent. In 1965, Negroes were 89.4 percent, all others, 10.6 percent. Schools that were predominantly Negro were crowded, sometimes on double shifts, while many white schools were half empty. Resegregation had occurred, the courts and the government notwithstanding.

Table 4. Cities with 200,000 or more Negroes

City	Total population	Negroes			Percent Negro
		Total	Males	Females	
New York, N.Y.	7,781,984	1,087,931	498,167	589,764	14.0
Chicago, Ill.	3,550,404	812,637	387,718	424,919	22.9
Philadelphia, Penn.	2,002,512	529,240	250,256	278,984	26.4
Detroit, Mich.	1,670,144	482,223	232,829	249,394	28.9
Washington, D.C.	763,956	411,737	196,257	215,480	53.9
Los Angeles, Calif.	2,479,015	334,916	160,118	174,798	13.5
Baltimore, Md.	939,024	325,589	157,130	168,459	34.7
Cleveland, Ohio	876,050	250,818	120,873	129,945	28.6
New Orleans, La.	627,525	233,514	110,096	123,418	37.2
Houston, Texas	938,219	215,037	103,471	111,566	22.9
St. Louis, Mo.	750,026	214,377	100,159	114,218	28.6

A Sampling of Other Cities

City	Total population	Total	Males	Females	Percent Negro
Pittsburgh, Penn.	604,332	100,692	48,670	52,022	16.7
Kansas City, Mo.	475,539	83,146	39,723	43,423	17.5
Boston, Mass.	697,197	63,165	30,081	33,084	9.1
Rochester, N.Y.	318,611	23,586	11,491	12,095	7.4
Minneapolis, Minn.	482,872	11,785	5,792	5,993	2.4

SOURCE: U.S. Census of Population: 1960.
Tables 4 and 5 are from *Dark Ghetto,* by Kenneth B. Clark, 1965. Data prepared by James Jones, Research Director of Haryou. Used by permission of Harper & Row.

One of the great population changes in modern history has been the movement of the Negro population from South to North and from country to city. Half a century ago, in 1910, eight out of ten Negroes lived in one of the eleven states of the old Confederacy. More than 90 percent of them lived in rural areas. Negroes began moving to the

North during World War I and continued to move during the 1920's when restrictive legislation slowed down the flow of immigrants from southern and eastern Europe. By 1940, the Negro population of the old Confederacy had increased only 12 percent; in the same period the Negro population elsewhere in the United States had more than doubled, from 1.9 million to four million. But the old Confederacy still held more than two-thirds of all U.S. Negroes.

Between 1940 and 1960, the Negro population outside of the old Confederacy increased two and one-quarter times, from nearly four million to more than nine million, or 48 percent of the total U.S. Negro population. In the eleven states of the old Confederacy, by contrast, Negro population grew only 9 percent. Most of the increase outside the South occurred in the central cities of the twelve largest U.S. metropolitan areas—New York, Los Angeles, Chicago, Philadelphia, Detroit, San Francisco-Oakland, Boston, Pittsburgh, St. Louis, Washington, Cleveland, Baltimore—which now hold more than 31 percent of all U.S. Negroes. In the last decade, there has been additional diffusion from big to smaller cities such as Buffalo, Rochester, Newark, New Haven, Fort Wayne, and San Diego.

Within the old Confederacy, Negro as well as white population has been shifting from the country to the city. The number of Negroes declined in the rural areas as the proportion living in cities jumped from 21 percent in 1940 (and 7 percent in 1910) to 41 percent in 1960. The Negro population of Dallas and Houston, for example, went up two and one-half times, and 75 percent in Atlanta and Miami.*

Carl E. Thronblad, Research Coordinator for the Research Council of the Great Cities Program for school improvement, has shown that:

1. In all the great cities, the proportion of the population that is white decreased from 1950 to 1960.
2. In all but three of the fifteen great cities the white population decreased, and in one of the three cases in which the white population increased, the increase from the period 1950 to 1960 was less than the increase from the period from 1940 to 1950.
3. In all of the fifteen great cities, the proportion of the population

---

* Charles E. Silberman, "The City and the Negro," *Fortune*, March, 1962.

that is nonwhite has increased since 1950 and in all but one case, a steady increase has been maintained since 1940.

4. In all cities, the nonwhite population has increased in number and, in all but one, the increase from 1950 to 1960 was 40 percent greater. The only exception was a 23 percent increase in the nonwhite population.

5. Analysis of age groups indicates that white children born in the city tend to leave the city before entering school or at least during their early elementary years. Following one group, those under five years old in 1950, through to the 1960 Census—the ten-to-fourteen-year age group in 1960—showed that the group decreased by more than 24 percent in eleven of the fifteen cities.

6. The same age group analysis in every case showed a larger decrease in the younger white age group than in the total white population, indicating that white families with children of elementary school age were tending to leave the central city in greater numbers than other white people.

The data suggest that if the trend continues the nation can expect a much smaller percentage of public school children in central cities to be white than is now the case. Because of increasing private school enrollment, especially of white children in the cities, the proportion of white students in the public schools can be expected to decrease.

In Philadelphia, in 1950, 27 percent of the nonwhite population lived in areas that were primarily nonwhite. Ten years later 58 percent lived in fairly solidly segregated neighborhoods. Only "token" whites remained. In the central city apartment and town house area, new building attracted whites back to town but the average age of those returning was sixty and had little effect on the concentrated Negro school population.

In New York, Negro school enrollment has gone up 67 percent in the past seven years. White enrollment declined 13 percent to less than half of the total school population. In the elementary grades, Negroes and Puerto Ricans are now a majority (50.8 percent). As the New York *Herald Tribune* pointed out (June 8, 1965), "a large part of white pupils left in the city has been drained off into parochial and other private schools, which enroll now about 29 percent of all school children. Of these 425,000 pupils in non-public schools in the city,

more than 90 percent are white." State Commissioner of Education
James E. Allen, Jr., expects nonwhite to total 66 percent of the public
school population in 1970 and 70 percent in 1975 (in Manhattan it is
already 73 percent).

In fifteen years, Negroes may be in the majority not only in Wash-

Table 5. Negro residential concentration by areas of cities

City and Area	Population	Negroes	Percent
New York, N.Y.			
Brooklyn area	91,391	87,654	95.9
Queens area	20,324	19,091	93.9
Manhattan area	241,125	236,051	97.9
Los Angeles, Calif.			
Area I	48,806	46,865	96.0
Area II	15,489	14,990	96.8
Baltimore, Md.			
Area I	149,197	143,849	96.4
Washington, D.C.			
Area I	120,060	115,552	96.2
Area II	66,043	64,196	97.2
Cleveland, Ohio			
Area I	70,060	68,700	98.1
Area II	49,815	46,863	94.1
St. Louis, Missouri			
Area I	97,144	93,807	96.6
New Orleans, Louisiana			
Area I	45,111	44,044	97.6
Chicago, Illinois			
Area I	347,806	340,599	97.9
Area II	105,307	102,096	97.0
Area III	21,133	20,401	96.5
Area IV	22,168	21,347	96.3

SOURCE: U.S. Census of Population: 1960.

ington, where they already are, but in Detroit, Baltimore, Cleveland,
Chicago, and St. Louis—and in twenty-five years in Philadelphia as
well. This would mean that of America's ten largest cities only three
(New York, New Orleans, and Houston) would have white majorities
(and the Borough of Manhattan would have a Negro majority). The

school population would show an even greater imbalance if the trend is not reversed, for most Negroes cannot now afford to withdraw from the public school system; many whites can. Approximately 90 percent of American children today attend segregated schools.

The nation in effect does not have a truly public school system in a large part of its communities; it has permitted what is in effect a private school system to develop under public auspices. It was no secret in the 1940's and 1950's that differences in quality of schools existed between a slum and Scarsdale. The nation knew about the Negro, but it kept its eyes shut, and its heart as well, for there is more than one way to know a fact and until the nation, spurred by the civil rights movement, began to know this fact emotionally as well as intellectually, there could be little commitment to abolish educational inequities.

The solution to *de facto* segregation, of course, is far more elusive than merely to require legal desegregation. The problem is what kind of governmental powers or interpositions Americans are prepared to take. What kind of freedoms are we prepared as a society to restrict or even eliminate?

A basic question is the freedom to move: the freedom to negotiate, to purchase homes, or to go somewhere else for the sake of job or children or way of life. America is hesitant to tamper with that freedom. It is hesitant also to tamper with local management of school districts. Since the end of the Second World War, the educational system has been under sharp attack from many for lack of quality education. The onslaught would have been far more fierce if competitive school systems around the country had not made it possible for those with the means and ambition to move out to the suburbs where the best teachers and the best programs often were to be found. Those with the greater economic capacity satisfied their needs and their own children's needs by moving to the Newtons, the Scarsdales, and the Grosse Pointes.

If such flexibility had not been built into this system, if they had not been able to move, if they had not had the freedom either of the private school or the next thing to it (that is, moving to a "good" suburb and paying tuition indirectly via high tax rates and mortgage payments), the social pressures might not have been absorbed. The fact that families of economic capacity were able to move eased pressure from the top—but it also widened their distance from the 20 percent of the poor at the bottom. This gap between the haves and have-nots became the social danger in the 1950's that caused James B. Conant to use the phrase—as accurate as it was telling—"social dynamite."

Control today over the quality of schools is, therefore, in good part a factor of residence, and control over place of residence is dependent on money and on race. But the freedom of mobility, which Americans cherish, is not available to all. Those on their way up in the society have freedom of choice of residence; those who are not have the slums. The freedom of some to move therefore conflicts with equality of opportunity. In recent years, we have accelerated and improved the education of that class which already ranked highest in educational attainment. The school systems of wealthy suburbia have prospered, attracting the best teachers and practicing the latest of curriculum improvements fashioned by scholars. But many of the schools of the cities have deteriorated relatively. And the children of these schools have declined relatively in achievement.

A mythology has spread in past decades as a balm to conscience— that slum children were somehow of a lower order of capacity than children in other sectors of our economy. This myth was aided by such labels—usually used with good intent—as "culturally deprived" and "socially underprivileged," or "disadvantaged." While the labels generally did describe the social and economic backgrounds of these children—as contrasted with middle class culture—far too often these labels became alibis for failure to find effective ways to educate these children. A correlate of the myth was that the children of poverty and racial minorities were not merely difficult to teach, but were virtually unteachable. It was true that they came from families of low educational attainment and that their homes lacked books and other incentives to learning. But this dreary recital was also used as an excuse for poor schools, poor teachers, and ineffective education. Such a mythology becomes self-fulfilling in schools of poverty. Standing apart from the community they serve, these slum schools slammed their doors shut at three-thirty when school closed for the day; thus the school was presumably "protected" from the neighborhood. In such schools, where the child was considered ungifted, the most dangerous gap in our society was permitted to grow and enlarge.

We are now engaged in new measures to end the fortress school, to

Chart 3. Median equivalent grades in reading comprehension for Central Harlem and New York City pupils compared to national norms

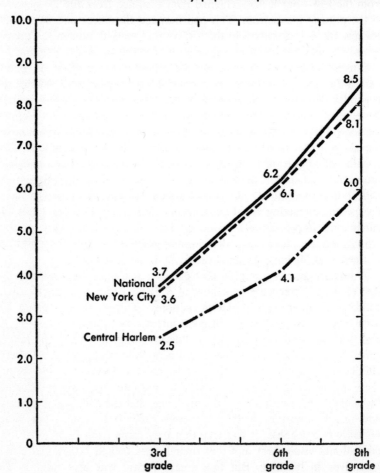

SOURCE: Prepared for *Youth in the Ghetto: A Study of the Consequences of Powerlessness and a Blueprint for Change*, Harlem Youth Opportunities Unlimited, Inc., p. 190.

bring to the children of poverty the more skilled of teachers, not the less skilled; the least crowded of classrooms, not the most crowded; the best of educational opportunity, not the least of it. But we are still at the beginning of the struggle. It cannot succeed unless equality of educational opportunity is a genuine national commitment securing, as President Johnson intends, priorities in American public policy.

By 1965 the facts of neglect were dramatized sufficiently to arouse the concern of many: that a brilliant but poor student had far less of a chance at college than an ordinary but well-to-do student; that a Negro child—despite his "disadvantaged background" that he had presumably brought to school in the beginning—found his IQ scores *declining* every year he remained in school; that a good teacher was inclined to avoid the difficult class where teaching talent was most needed, in preference for the easier class of the children of the comfortable.

The problems—and the threat to democracy—were identified. The relevant question has become what to do about it.

One can start at either end—abolish poverty, segregation, oppression, the conditions on which neglect feeds, or ameliorate the conditions by improving the schools in the midst of poverty and prejudice. There is harsh conflict as to the choice between those who will settle for nothing less than the transformation of society and those who either do not wish to transform society or are skeptical about the immediate possibility.

The answer is that both goals—the abolition of the conditions of neglect and the improvement of the schools—have to be achieved together. If a Negro can never escape the ghetto of inferior employment, segregated housing, and a sense of racial inferiority, money poured into ghetto schools may lead only to increased bitterness and frustration. On the other hand, if the schools wait for the transformation of society to set their own house in order, new generations of children will be lost. The schools are part of the society which must be transformed. Teachers who patronize the poor and the Negro, and school boards which allow education to deteriorate in the slums are as responsible a factor in perpetuating inferiority of performance as the broken and crowded homes from which the children come. For too long the schools have blamed the community

Chart 4. Median IQ scores for Central Harlem and New York City pupils compared to national norms

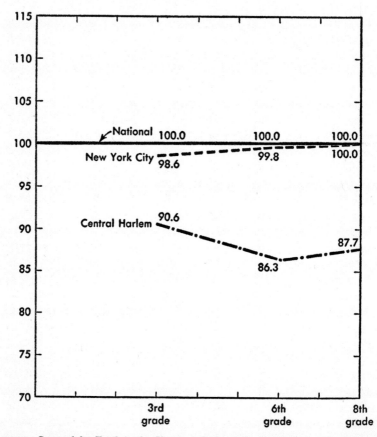

SOURCE: Prepared for *Youth in the Ghetto: A Study of the Consequences of Powerlessness and a Blueprint for Change,* 1964, Harlem Youth Opportunities Unlimited, Inc., p. 193.

IQ tests, originally believed to assess innate intellectual capacity, are now understood to be influenced by cultural and educational opportunities. Whatever the weaknesses of these scores as a test of intelligence, the above chart does show that the "capacity" of children in Central Harlem declines between the third and sixth grades, rising slightly between the sixth and eighth grades, while the scores of children in New York City as a whole rise slightly from grades three to eight.

and the community has blamed the schools, as though they were not one and the same. If a Negro child is "deprived," his deprivation *includes* the school.

Until the schools in the slums and on the edges of the slums are as good as the schools in ambitious suburbia, it is hard if not impossible to prevent the exodus of the middle class from the city and/or from the public school system. The ghetto and the poor schools will both have to go. Full national development, in an economic sense, cannot be based on pockets of poverty and social neglect.

Open enrollment—allowing parents to send their children to another school—has not, by the mid-1960's, proved itself an adequate solution to the problems of desegregation in either North or South, when considered apart from other measures. It has been attacked by civil rights leaders as tending to encourage the belief that it is a substitute for organized reform and as tending to put the burden of social change upon the individual who, in many communities, is understandably afraid to take the risk of such independent action. Other means had then to be found which could solve the differing residential and economic realities of segregation in American urban life.

In a country where education is traditionally the concern of the local community and of the state, the federal government alone cannot bring out the desired social change. Federal funds can help to train or retrain teachers for service in urban schools; they can aid in the establishment of educational parks and other programs designed not only to consolidate school resources more economically but to transcend the geographic boundaries of urban ghettos. Federal funds can help raise the quality of these schools through appropriations for better salaries, smaller classes, more efficient equipment, more adequate libraries and laboratories. By making grants to scholars and teachers they can encourage the writing of more adequate textbooks, more up-to-date, more comprehensive, and more reflective of the society as it is—far too many texts used in these schools have been out of date and have pictured the American family only as white, and as a resident of a small town or suburb.

As it has through the antipoverty program, the federal government can support plans like Head Start, designed to give the preschool children of the poor some of the advantages of health care, of exposure to language and books which the children of the more privileged normally receive. Yet such programs will falter—and may even cause greater disillusionment—if they are not followed by "quality education" in the schools themselves. A child prepared to read at five must be taught to read at six or the preparation is wasted.

Only the local communities can make clear the commitment to the combination of integrated and high-quality education which will heighten the morale and dedication of teachers and administrators of

Chart 5. Percentage of 3-, 4-, and 5-year-olds enrolled in nursery schools and kindergarten, by family income: October, 1964

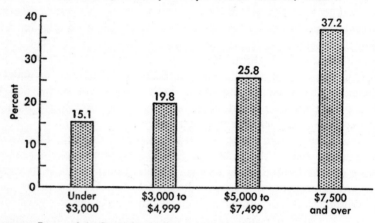

SOURCE: Bureau of the Census for the Office of Education.

urban schools. Commitment is contagious and so is the lack of it.

Many steps can be taken in the local communities to save their human resources. Minority groups require representation in administrative and policy positions in the schools, and on elected or appointed school boards. Some of the current programs suggested, however, are panaceas; "busing" and the neighborhood school issue can become, for example, peripheral questions which divert attention from the primary goals of improving the schools themselves. Some of the most important steps to be taken involve the teacher, both as to attitude and training. The task is not hopeless, as the history of the education of generations of immigrants has shown. Neither is it easy, for the cultures, the vocabulary, the mores of teacher and pupil are often far apart. A child who seems withdrawn and unteachable may merely be retreating from what seems to him an unfriendly face or an unfamiliar setting. Many a teacher who wishes to teach a child from the slums has to reach out now across an abyss of culture and condition. Some of the idealism of the Peace Corps is needed here, and a great deal of that sense of justice and fairness which can characterize an American community when its conscience is aroused. And there can be no doubt that the time has come to arouse that conscience in the cities.

At present, slum schools have the youngest, least experienced teachers, and their turnover is high. It is scarcely surprising that children in such schools do not learn. Yet teachers reluctant to teach in the slum schools protest rightly about the quality of such schools. They do not want to teach in schools where walls are cracked and dirty, where windows are broken, where libraries are poorly equipped or nonexistent, where classes are crowded, and where administrators seem defeatist. For the teacher's sake—but ultimately and primarily for the child's—the quality of these schools must be brought up to the level of the best schools. Yet faith in children's capacity to learn is a greater factor in their eventual success than is the condition of the plaster on the walls, or even the quality of the textbooks. Such faith is shown not by the educational system alone, but by the standards and behavior of the society as a whole.

Even in schools that have been successfully "integrated," however, the Negro and the poor may be effectively separated from others and become the victims of inadequate and unequal education. We still have no reliable tests to measure innate intellectual potential untainted by cultural limitations. An IQ test emphasizing vocabulary familiar to children of the well-to-do, but unfamiliar to others, will rank children falsely in terms of mental capacity. The danger, which is real, is that a pupil will become "typed" as bright or dull early in life and will be so regarded by his teachers—and what is just as bad, by himself—when in fact he may have unplumbed talent. The danger is the arbitrary limitation of possibilities. Too often students have been nudged into narrow vocational courses merely because of assumptions of restricted future opportunities. Custodial care can and has in effect taken the place of education under such circumstances. Yet there are experimental programs which indicate that the dedication of the teacher can transform the "unteachable" child.

By whatever means children are organized in an individual school —and, of course, they must be organized in some manner—they need not be divided so that the ends of education itself are defeated. Similarly, if the creative student is held to mediocrity, the loss is irreparable to the individual and to society as well. Ways must be found to sacrifice neither equality nor quality in the necessary revolution in American education.

The solution to *de facto* segregation presumably will not come tomorrow, for every society has many techniques for avoiding painful change. There is a gap between public and private morality, between public statement of ethics and private performance. Yet our history brings confidence that there is not so wide a gap in the moral arc but that the electricity can cross. The first step is clear. A major improvement in the quality of both urban and rural schools for the poor is essential, as the Allen Committee report made clear in its analysis of the New York City school situation. At least some of the reasons why the white people have moved out, or indeed why the Negro intellectual also has left the cities, are related to the fact that the schools are simply not good and they know it. And there is little sense in arguing that this first step is not worth taking unless a lot of other steps are taken as well if true equality of opportunity is to be won. If not a sufficient condition, it is at least a necessary condition.

Most leaders in education think that to wait patiently for a transformation of conscience on the part of families is to wait too long. They point out that it is to expect more than most persons will be willing to give to the cause of racial justice to expect the "advantaged" to "sacrifice their children" by keeping them in inferior public schools in urban areas. Educational policy, the sardonic observer may point out, is designed for other people's children. The more practical approach, however, is to see to it that slum schools, urban or rural, are not inferior, indeed that they are superior. If education of high quality and integrated education are joined, not only could urban Negroes move rapidly out of the depressed class, but many white families might very well give up the financial burden of private school tuition

Table 6. Changing white attitudes toward school desegregation

"Do you think white students and Negro students should go to the same schools or to separate schools?"*

	Percentage Answering "Same Schools"		
	1942	1956	1963
White Northerners	40	61	73
White Southerners	2	14	34
Total Whites	30	49	63

"Would you yourself have any objection to sending your children to a school *where a few of the children are colored?*"**

	Percentage Answering "No, would not object"	
	1963	1965
White Northern Parents	87	91
White Southern Parents	38	62

". . . where half of the children are colored?"

White Northern Parents	56	65
White Southern parents	17	27

". . . where more than half of the children are colored?"

White Northern Parents	31	37
White Southern Parents	6	16

* Studies conducted by National Opinion Research Center and reported in: H. H. Hyman and P. B. Sheatsley, "Attitudes Toward Desegregation," *Scientific American*, July 1964, *211*, 16–23.
** Studies conducted by the American Institute of Public Opinion and reported in: G. Gallup's press release of May 22, 1965.

or high mortgages and return to the public schools of the cities. Some of the white middle class might thus be retrieved for the cities from the suburbs. The realist must report that without adoption of some such strategy it is likely that the gap between classes and races will steadily widen. Not only American institutions but the American character is being put to the test by the struggle for equal and excellent education for all. May we not ask ourselves, in Jaeger's language, What is the American's "active awareness of a standard" in matters of discrimination? What are the values to which we are committed?

Educators can make a major contribution by driving to raise quality, particularly in the slum schools. For the over-all social health of the United States, as the Congress wisely decided in the Elementary and Secondary Education Act of 1965 (see Appendix B), the nation must provide more money relatively to those schools than to the rest of the community. But to put the burden of racial integration of schools on the educators alone, or the federal government alone, is to misjudge the American style and the American way of doing things— and the facts. If city schools are to change, real estate boards will have to play a role comparable to school boards. City government will have to join hands with school management. A social revolution is not made by any one section of society; many hands must join if the wheel is to turn.

An essential move, of course, is the change in the nature of city life. President Johnson in a message to the Congress in January, 1966, stated the problem in these terms:

We know the convenience of city life, and its paralysis. We know its promise, and its dark foreboding. What we may only dimly perceive is the gravity of the choice before us. Shall we make our cities livable for ourselves and our posterity? Or shall we by timidity and neglect damn them to fester and decay?

If we permit our cities to grow without rational design; if we stand passively by, while the center of each can become a hive of depravation, crime, and hopelessness; if we devour the countryside as though it were limitless, while our ruins—millions of tenement apartments and dilapidated houses—go unredeemed; if we become two people, the suburban affluent and the urban poor, each filled with mistrust and fear one for the other—if this is our desire and policy as a people, then we shall effectively cripple each generation to come. We shall as well condemn our own generation to a bitter paradox: an educated, wealthy, progressive people, who would not give their thoughts, their resources, or their wills to provide for their common well-being.

I do not believe such a fate is either necessary or inevitable. But I believe this will come to pass—unless we commit ourselves now to the planning, the building, the teaching, and the caring that alone can forestall it. That is why I am recommending today a massive demonstration cities program. I recommend that both the public and private sectors of our economy join to build in our cities and towns an environment for man equal to the dignity of his aspirations.

The schools must be part of such a program. They cannot be considered apart from metropolitan planning, or from housing developments, or from transportation. Indeed, the hope of reviving the schools of the American city rests as much or more on the actions of the leaders of finance and commerce as it does on the actions of the educators, who are rarely at the center of the power structure. It is to the self-interest of both business and education to join forces in remaking the city schools. If they do not, the future of public education in the rest of this century is in doubt, and the very success of the American way of life is in jeopardy.

IV Human Resources and the National Interest

A new influence affected national thinking about education in the early 1960's: the idea that education is a factor in economic growth, that human resources can be conceived as economic resources, as a national treasure to be conserved and developed for the public good.

When soil was eroded by flood or drought, when timberland was destroyed and not replaced, the nation learned to deplore the waste of natural resources and moved to action with conservation programs, but only recently has the nation discovered that some of the most precious of all its natural resources—human beings—have been neglected for generations.

Yet educators for generations have made this point to anyone who would listen. There has been no lack of rhetoric. But the educator's voice was heard usually at the local level. It was not until Russian scientific successes and domestic social problems brought the issue to a national focus that action became possible on a nationwide scale. Until that day, America tended to think of education as consumption rather than investment, as an individual good rather than the basis for an expanding economy. More attention by the national government was paid, therefore, to physical than to human resources.

The Office of Saline Water was established before anyone dreamed of an Office of Economic Opportunity. It has been said that more money was spent for migratory birds than for the children of migrant workers. The Cropland Conservation Program predates the Job Corps. Loans were authorized for agricultural conservation years before the

National Defense Education Act enabled loans to permit able but needy students the opportunity of higher education, and far more federal money has been spent in the past for forest brush disposal than for research on educational problems.

The nation in the 1960's came to see that waste in human resources was concentrated in those areas furthest removed from the center— the poor, the Negro, the brilliant and creative, the mentally retarded. Most Americans are none of these. Of normal intelligence, they are white, middle class, and unafflicted with physical handicaps. Yet not only do the nonaverage and the exceptional suffer from such neglect but the majority, too, suffer—without knowing it—from the lack of the counterstimulus of creative difference. It took the Russian competition and an economist's view to make the point clear.

"The education of our people is the most basic resource of our society . . . it is the most important force behind economic growth. . . ."

These words are from the President's Council of Economic Advisers in its annual report of 1965.

Such losses, put in cold-cash terms, accented the urgency for measures to repair those ruptures in the nation's social structure that caused such leakage of human resources. A principal tool at the nation's command was education. The schools, it was agreed, must carry the major burden of response by helping all young people to set out toward productive goals by providing the training necessary to achieve those goals.

Simply as a matter of economics, the nation apparently no longer proposed to tolerate the extravagance of education meted out unevenly because of family income or class or color or any other accident of birth—of scant or mediocre instruction for the poor or for members of minority groups, of failure to provide opportunities for women (a statistical majority, a social "minority"), or of careless neglect of those whose ability to learn happened to have been wrongly measured.

As a result, a noteworthy shift took place, a turn in the revolution of education toward greater concentration on human resources. In the federal budget for the fiscal year that ended June 30, 1965, total expenditures for agriculture, agricultural resources, and natural resources dropped from $8 billion for the previous year to $7.2 billion while the total expenditures for health, labor, welfare, and education rose from $6.8 billion in fiscal 1964 to $7.7 billion for 1965. Federal expenditures for the Office of Education alone moved from $1.5 billion in 1965 to $2.3 billion in 1966. The balance shifted also from material to human within the field of education. More than a half of the total federal expenditures for education in 1935 went for brick-and-mortar school construction rather than for school services. This ratio dropped to about 15 percent by 1964 with wholesome effect on the amount of attention focused on the individual student.

The federal government made a further commitment to the conservation of human resources and the curtailment of their waste. The Civil Rights Act of 1964 was designed as an instrument for making sure that no youngster was denied equal educational opportunities. And the Elementary and Secondary Education Act of 1965 extended a helping hand to virtually every school district of the nation. These were among an array of legislative acts representing a major breakthrough toward bringing better-quality education at all levels within reach of all of the people.

But these could only be the beginning. Much remained to be done if the nation was to secure for its present and future the assurance that each child would have the kind or amount of education that would serve him and the nation to the extent required by national goals and by the vexing challenges from abroad. Again let us look at the facts and projections.

Between 1965 and 1975, approximately thirty million young men and women will leave school to embark upon the adventure of looking for their first jobs. Unless current projections are changed by conscious action of federal, state, and local action, at least two million of these youngsters may never enter high school and at least another seven million may not receive a diploma. And many may therefore find no jobs. Skill obsolescence affects the youth most of all. A Department of Labor survey in October, 1964, found 695,000 unemployed dropouts and graduates aged sixteen to twenty-one.

Thus very nearly a third of the crop of this American resource will—unless the necessary revolution occurs remarkably soon—be unprepared to make the contribution to the economy that the nation

Table 7. Relationship between level of schooling and family income, United States (percentage distribution of families, by level of schooling of family heads) :1963

Level of schooling	Income under $2,000	All families
Total	100	100
Elementary:		
Less than 8 years	38	15
8 years	23	18
High school:		
1 to 3 years	17	19
4 years	14	28
College	8	20

SOURCE: Census P60, No. 43, p. 25, table 7.

High school seniors from families with $12,000 or more annual income have a 74 percent chance of graduating in the top half of their class; those from families with $6,000 to $9,000 annual income have a 68 percent chance of graduating in the top half of their class; but those from families with less than $3,000 annual income only have a 45 percent chance of graduating in the top half of their class.

SOURCE: U.S. Office of Education, Cooperative Research Study: Project Talent; Final Report for Cooperative Research Project No. 635, pp. 11–20.

is coming to expect. Surely more important, they may well individually lead unsatisfying and drab lives, confined to uninteresting jobs and inadequate wages.

In regard to the training for jobs, much could be said about vocational education that is beyond the boundaries of this book, for vocational and technical education is under intense scrutiny in educational and industrial circles. In an age of automation and rapid industrial change, it is difficult for vocational schools themselves to avoid quick obsolescence. There is the possibility that the comprehensive high school—which brings together young people of all backgrounds and a variety of abilities, some on their way to college, others on their way directly into industry—may be the most viable school for a democratic society in a rapidly changing economy. It may well be that vocational and technical schools in the future will prove most useful by following secondary education, as many programs have started to do. They can serve as institutes both for prior training for skilled jobs and for the continued education of men and women whose previously learned skills have become out of date. The need for such opportunities has already been demonstrated by the Manpower and Development Training Program financed by the federal government and by the programs established by many large industries.

The brilliant and creative student—in the aftermath of Sputnik— received more and more attention, which both he and the society required. But the society has come to realize that there was another area of need, and a more tragic waste, in this plight of the poor. We have looked earlier at the facts of their schooling. Yet statistics alone can not reveal how perpetuation of poverty and of ignorance breeds, in any part of the population, a rotting of the mind and spirit. There is a special irony, it seems to many, in the fact that when a man is out of a job for a year because he has not learned a skill, the cost to the nation in lost production is greater than the cost of sending a person

Table 8. Income from ages 25 to 64 and mean income of males 25 to 64 years old, by years of school completed: 1949, 1956, and 1961

(Beginning 1961, includes Alaska and Hawaii. Figures for lifetime income based on application of appropriate life tables to arithmetic mean income, by age, as obtained for a cross section of population in each year shown. Figures for mean income for 1949 based on Census of Population data and, for 1956 and 1961, on Current Population Survey.)

Years of school completed	Income from ages 25 to 64			Mean income		
	1949	1956	1961	1949	1956	1961
Elementary:						
Less than 8 years[1]	$ 79,654	$108,310	$124,930	$2,232	$2,979	$3,483
8 years	106,889	148,033	168,810	2,988	4,079	4,750
High school:						
1 to 3 years	121,943	169,501	193,082	3,279	4,634	5,305
4 years	148,649	208,322	224,417	3,820	5,553	6,102
College:						
1 to 3 years	173,166	243,611	273,049	4,489	6,505	7,392
4 years or more	241,427	340,131	360,604	6,236	8,716	9,530

1 Includes males reporting no years of school completed.

SOURCE: American Economic Association, *The American Economic Review*, December 1960; and Department of Commerce, Bureau of the Census, unpublished data.

to school for twelve years. The cost of the crime, the drug addiction and delinquency, and the broken and dependent homes of uneducated persons is far greater than the cost of good education would have been.

For reasons buried deep in American history, including the fact that education was not mentioned in the Constitution, the carrying out of the ideal of equality of educational opportunity was left to the several states, but despite valiant efforts in many parts of the country to create such equality, the facts are distressingly clear: As a nation we have not succeeded. The interests of the nation, which can be expected to benefit from the development of the talents of all its children, and those of the individual and his family, can be expected to merge. But the machinery of government is only now adjusting to making this merger possible for education as it did, for example, support the tie between the interests of the citizen and the nation for the common defense. No foreseeable change in the economic life of the nation to make feasible provision of equality of opportunity throughout the land from the resources of the states and communities alone now seems likely. The nation faces a situation in which two sets of interests—the individual and the national—can be in conflict with the pattern of local and state capacity.

Let us consider, for example, the federal interests in the talents of the younger generation. Until the Second World War it had been assumed by most people that all the skills needed for the proper management of the affairs of the nation would flow naturally from the operation of the schools and colleges. Government leaders and educators alike tended to assume that this was not an area of federal interest. Shortages of trained personnel in the Second World War, and during the succeeding decades, changed the minds of some government officials and some educators. The field of science particularly attracted their attention. The National Science Foundation, through federally supported fellowships, engaged actively in trying to influence the flow of students into these areas, and by other means tried to improve the quality of work of the schools in the teaching of science. The Departments of Defense and of Health, Education, and Welfare poured funds, largely at the college and university level, into teaching as well as into research programs in areas that seemed to the Congress important for national needs. Studies of the nation's needs for specialized personnel were encouraged by many agencies of government. In short, the movements for national support begun on a small scale in agriculture and vocational education by World War I had spread rapidly by the mid-1960's to most of the areas included in the curriculum of the schools and colleges. But the emphasis was in science and applied science. Finally, the 89th Congress in 1965 even lent support to the creative arts and to the humanities, on a scale that did not redress the imbalance between the arts and sciences but did affirm such a national commitment for the first time.

The historical record of the last hundred years suggests that with every social change come changes in educational policy. It is unrealistic to assume that any set of aims, whether local or federal, can be static. This fact forces us to think about the machinery by which future adaptations and decisions will be made. The plight of minority groups demonstrates that past methods have not been good enough. Imbalance between federal support of different parts of the educational world—the universities as compared with the small colleges, the sciences as compared with the arts—has also become a matter of public and professional concern. All such problems force us to realize that to determine the nature of the *process* of decision is in part to determine the nature of the policies themselves.

This is obviously the case in such an area as the high school curriculum. If, for example, the voice of the liberal arts college is to be given the greatest weight, one can predict that the program will be different from the one that would emerge if the voice of local business were given priority. And would either be sensitive to the voice of the poor? If the place of the professional educator is strengthened, it seems likely that the schools will expand their functions, for it is of the nature of the professional to assume that his skills can be applied to an ever-wider field of human endeavor. And so on, and so on, through the long list of groups and forces that have an interest in the educational institutions of the nation.

The very listing of these factors forces attention on the procedure of policy making. It forces attention on how best to direct social forces, on how to create from many sources of energy an instrument with a common goal. The model the nation seeks may not be unlike

Henry Adams' dynamo, a balance of motion and stability, of controlled power and the release of energy. More familiar to American thought, perhaps, is a model from the Constitutional Convention.

It is not unreasonable to appeal to the founders of the American system of government in considering a model for the making of educational policy. They proposed a plan of checks and balances for the system of government, as well as centers of power and initiative. More than any group in history the authors of the Constitution consciously created an instrument of government which by its internal workings was designed to avoid the excessive power of any one group or interest over any other, and yet was able to adjust to changing times. The energies of the several groups—economic, religious, social—were recognized. The differences of opinion which existed among the founders themselves about the needs for safeguards against anarchy—perhaps particularly about the relation of property to social stability—were themselves built into the engine of government. The competing yet cooperating branches of government, the legislative, executive, and judicial, were designed to form a single dynamo, not a series of unrelated machines. Hence in the Constitution it was necessary to spell out not only the functions of each but also the points at which each touched the others.

And checks and balances now exist in the relations among the local, state, and federal governments in the field of education. The provisions of federal and state constitutions place restraints upon local educational policy. As we have seen in recent years, the courts have had their profoundest influence in the areas of church and state, and race relations.

Perhaps the most knotty of the problems that have arisen is the relationship of the school to religious belief. For many parents—though by no means all—there is advantage in merging the teaching of the usual school subjects with instruction in religious matters. Indeed, for the greater part of the time since the first settlement of the colonies, this was accepted practice. Religion was originally part of the American school system. In 1647 the "Old Deluder Satan Act," passed in Massachusetts, provided that children be taught to read and write so they could study the Scriptures and thus avoid "ye ould deluder, Satan." The Church of England was the established religion in several colonies, and taxes were sometimes levied for its support. The schools were virtually all church schools, reflecting the religious beliefs of the Protestant majority. When public education made its appearance in America the various Protestant sects argued over the proper moral and religious training to be given in these free public schools. The decision was to maintain them as secular institutions, though Protestant-oriented practices, such as school prayers, Bible reading, celebration of religious holidays, and the like, were continued.

Parents of other religious groups began to consider an alternative to the public schools—their own parochial schools. The Catholic school system grew to enroll one-eighth of the American student population. Catholic parochial schools by mid-century included more than 90 percent of all nonpublic grade school and 80 percent of all nonpublic high school students. In 1940, there were 25.4 million children in public elementary and secondary schools, and nearly 2.4 million in Catholic schools. By 1960, the public enrollment had jumped to 36 million, and the Catholic enrollment to 5.2 million. By the end of the decade, it is estimated that the public schools will be up 75 percent over 1940, and Catholic enrollment about 170 percent.

Many parents of like mind in religious belief wanted, and many clearly still want, the schools to take responsibility for the teaching of religious tenets. The views of the Catholic citizen on this relationship of school to church is perhaps the best known to the public today, but the attitude is shared in certain Protestant and some Jewish groups.

Yet the American society as a whole, as expressed in the federal Constitution and in judicial decisions, and in the state constitutions, has taken a different position. The belief that a policy of separation of church and state would permit freedom of religious worship and, at the same time, free the state from disharmony, has deep roots in the nation's political life. Because the public schools represent the State, the courts again and again have ruled that the schools are included in the doctrine of separation. No other issue of educational policy has risen so often for decision at the high judicial level. In part as the result of this conflict, the most rapidly growing group of nonpublic schools are those under church auspices. The difference of view is clear, and in this area the national government, first through the courts and recently through legislation, has clearly formed policy affecting the schools.

In the wake of the defeat of a number of federal education bills in the 1950's and early 1960's, a new procedure was adopted in the hope of accommodating both interests. The Elementary and Secondary Education Act of 1965 provided support to programs under public school management for educationally disadvantaged children whether enrolled in public or private schools. "Shared time" or "dual enrollment" arrangements were thereby encouraged. Those dissatisfied with this formula said that religious schools were aided by being freed, to the extent that these programs helped their students, to use their hard-pressed funds for religious activities. Those pleased with the formula pointed out that the child, not the church, received the primary benefit and that the primary national concern was the child. In a democratic society, they argued, it is to the interest of society that Catholic or other students meet non-Catholics on a common ground, under public auspices. And there could be little doubt that the rubbing of shoulders in class as well as on the playing fields was in the national interest.

As this book goes to press the nation is embarked on an effort to put this new program, summarized in Appendix B, to work. Already it is clear that a few state constitutions, more stringent in language than the First Amendment of the federal Constitution, will present problems. Local cooperation between public and private schools is required, and thousands of communities have had to start from scratch. Yet the desire to improve all schooling, together with the ecumenical spirit springing from Pope John's initiative and the cooperation of church leaders on civil rights, gives reason for measured optimism that a new approach to solving an old problem of the relation of private to public school, of private concern to public interest, may be in the making, leading to local cooperation instead of conflict.

Six factors have to be considered in making educational policy: the children and their parents, the nature of what is to be taught, the community and state in which the children live, the educators, the needs of enterprises and groups of all sorts, and the national interest. Only recently have the national interest and the needs of the subjects

Table 9. Median school years completed by persons 25 years old and over, by region: 1960

Region	Both sexes, white and nonwhite	Male	Female	White	Nonwhite
United States	10.6	10.3	10.9	10.9	8.2
Northeast	10.7	10.5	10.8	10.8	9.2
North Central	10.7	10.3	11.0	10.8	9.0
South	9.6	9.1	9.9	10.4	7.1
West	12.0	11.8	12.1	12.1	10.0

SOURCE: U.S. Department of Commerce, Bureau of the Census, U.S. Census of Population: 1960, PC(1)IC.

to be taught been adequately weighed in the balance. The interests of parents and children, of the professional educators, of the community, and of special interest groups, on the other hand, seem to have a sufficient, indeed a governing, voice through the local school board or committee. For the great majority of Americans, who fear the centralization of power, this guarantee of local responsibility and initiative is a most precious possession—not to be given up or challenged any more than the independence of the judiciary is challenged.

No formula is available for the proper balance and mixture of the forces which should influence educational policy, local and state and federal and private. What seems appropriate today may seem unwise tomorrow. The schools are so closely linked with society that development in one area of the economy will affect other areas. The requirements of national defense may call for rapid training in some specialties, while at another time the reduction of working hours may call for a more leisurely education in cultural subjects. The problem here is not what the precise policy shall be, but rather how shall decision on that policy be reached.

By sheer necessity of distance and poor communication the first schools had to be managed by the local people. It was neither possible nor probably thought wise to set up a central system of management. As communities grew and direction and inspection became possible, the area of local administration was expanded but only to make possible better tax bases or more complete services to the student. When the authors of the Constitution, by omitting reference to education, left it up to the states to proceed as they wished in the matter, they in practice also assured that local control as established in the first colonies would be carried on by the new states admitted into the Union. For what models could they have had to use other than those first established in Massachusetts and Virginia? Jefferson's thinking about the nature of government has influenced the schools as profoundly as his views on education itself. His sense of the importance of the family and of nearness to the elements of life has lent powerful support to the pattern of local control for more than a century after his death. If the first settlements had been both nearer to each other and congenial to the notion of centralized government, the pattern of education would have been different, but they were not.

The first links in educational policy were to the church and the community, and as the ties to the first were slowly separated, the ties to the second were strengthened by successive state governments. In some areas geography required different political structures: local social situations in practice put the control in the hands of different groups. But the grand pattern was and is similar enough so that a superintendent of schools today can be moved to California from Maine, or a college president from Florida to Hawaii, without the major shift in orientation that would be required if he moved to a position in France or Italy or even England. The fact that educational policy was derived from local authority did not therefore lead to the discrepancy in program one might imagine. The very fact that the local governments are similar in style has tended to create a near uniformity of approach. Three additional forces have bound the elementary and secondary schools together: the educational associations, the teachers' colleges and schools of education of the universities, and the publishing firms and other groups which provide the classroom materials. Each works directly with local and state school systems, but most are also concerned with regional and national groups. Under their auspices, teachers and administrators are in constant touch with others in the profession, and increasingly with citizens who make up the local school boards. Ideas about education are given wide circulation. They have acted as conservative forces, both in the sense of conservation of tradition and, all too often, in the sense of resistance to change. But also they have given a "national" character to American education.

While the competition among the states making up the Union is no longer the issue that it was at the time of founding the nation, certain factors still require that the voice of the state as a unit be heard in the making of educational policies. To begin with, the economic life of the states differ one from another. Some are primarily agricultural, some primarily industrial. For some the financing of education is manageable. For others the support of public schools is a major difficulty. Some have problems of cultural relations with those of other traditions, such as the Southwestern states with Mexicans and the Northeastern states with the French groups who crossed the borders from Canada. The differences in views between the Southern and the Northern states in the matter of racially segregated schools have already been noted. A further difference exists in the competition between these areas. All of these factors have an impact on the curricula of the schools as well as on the amount of the wealth which a particular state wishes to invest in education. State interests do not necessarily coincide with the interests of the family or of the national government.

The key issue in the relationship of local, state, and federal governments in education has come to be whether other than local influences or restraints can be brought to bear on school boards without endangering their capacity for initiative and responsibility. The answer is clearly "yes." Experience at all levels of government suggests that coequal and independent units can combine their efforts if the ground rules are clear. And experience with local school boards shows that despite state control over such factors as the certification of personnel, the kinds of buildings, and the like, and despite federal programs, and despite the Civil Rights Act, basic operating control is still in local hands.

The citizen must recall, as Diodorus wrote, that "in practice, none of the supposed blessings of life is ever granted to human beings in its entirety, and none of the evil occurs in an absolute form without an admixture of good." For if the American people, and particularly their educators, are optimists when it comes to the nature of man, they

Table 10. Gross national product related to total expenditures[1] for education: United States, selected years from 1929 to 1964

Calendar year	Gross national product	School year	Expenditures for education Total	As a percent of gross national product
1929	$103,095,000,000	1929–30	$3,233,601,000	3.1
1931	75,820,000,000	1931–32	2,966,464,000	3.9
1933	55,601,000,000	1933–34	2,294,896,000	4.1
1935	72,247,000,000	1935–36	2,649,914,000	3.7
1937	90,446,000,000	1937–38	3,014,074,000	3.3
1939	90,494,000,000	1939–40	3,199,593,000	3.5
1941	124,540,000,000	1941–42	3,203,548,000	2.6
1943	191,592,000,000	1943–44	3,522,007,000	1.8
1945	212,010,000,000	1945–46	4,167,597,000	2.0
1947	231,323,000,000	1947–48	6,574,379,000	2.8
1949	256,484,000,000	1949–50	8,795,635,000	3.4
1951	328,404,000,000	1951–52	11,312,446,000	3.4
1953	364,593,000,000	1953–54	13,949,876,000	3.8
1955	397,960,000,000	1955–56	16,811,651,000	4.2
1957	441,134,000,000	1957–58	21,119,565,000	4.8
1959	483,650,000,000	1959–60	24,722,464,000	5.1
1961	520,109,000,000	1961–62	29,366,305,000	5.6
1963	589,238,000,000	1963–64	[2]35,900,000,000	6.1
1964	628,699,000,000	1964–65	[2]39,000,000,000	6.2

1 Includes expenditures of public and nonpublic schools at all levels of education (elementary, secondary, and higher education).

2 Estimated.

NOTE: Beginning with 1959–60 school year, includes Alaska and Hawaii.

SOURCES: U.S. Department of Health, Education, and Welfare, Office of Education, *Biennial Survey of Education in the United States; Statistics of State School Systems; Financial Statistics of Institutions of Higher Education;* and unpublished data. U.S. Department of Commerce, Office of Business Economics, Survey of Current Business, August, 1965.

are pessimists when it comes to resting too much authority for educational policy in any place or person. As an individual, man may learn to be good, but beware of his susceptibility to social evil, beware of his tendency to acquire power over others. To restrain that tendency has been one of the major concerns of those formulating educational policy.

Where reforms have been proposed, they were stated in terms of the improvement of local units either by enlargement to assure efficiency

Table 11. Total and per-pupil expenditures for public elementary and secondary education: United States, selected years from 1919–1920 to 1964–65

School year	Total	Total expenditure per pupil in average daily attendance
1919–20	$ 1,036,151,000	$ 64
1920–30	2,316,790,000	108
1939–40	2,344,049,000	106
1949–50	5,837,643,000	259
1951–52	7,344,237,000	313
1953–54	9,092,449,000	351
1955–56	10,955,047,000	388
1957–58	13,569,163,000	449
1959–60	15,613,255,000	472
1961–62	18,373,339,000	518
1963–64	21,444,434,000	562
1964–65[1]	23,106,854,000	587
1965–66	25,801,995,000	641

1 Estimated.

NOTE: Beginning in 1959–60, includes Alaska and Hawaii.

SOURCE: U.S. Department of Health, Education, and Welfare, Office of Education, *Statistics of State School Systems, 1963–64;* and *Fall Statistics of Public Schools, 1964 and 1965.*

or by different means of financing to provide better services. Such reforms were often accompanied by the argument that their accomplishment would reduce the chances of more central control. Until recently, it has been assumed that the whole enterprise must be kept clear of "politics"—by which was meant the type of politics which would involve linking party platforms about which there was dispute, and party patronage, with the schools. The two ideas—platforms and patronage—were not often separated. Until the last few years, as a result, the schools have not been associated in the public mind with the great issues of the time, such as foreign policy, or government's relation to business or labor, or the development of electric power. The principal influence on legislatures, whether state or national, had been left to the educators themselves. Public opinion about the inadequacy of the schools was aroused by the educators, not by the politicians. Yet this anomaly has received relatively little comment from those who might have been expected to be concerned—politicians or their academic Boswells, the political scientists.

One may guess that national political leaders were not active in education until the 1950's because there seemed little advantage and some risk in taking leadership. The role of the federal government had not been defined, and the relationship of federal, state, and local authorities was in dispute. Only those projects about which there was little dispute received support at the national level: vocational education, agricultural schools, free luncheons, education for veterans, and the like. State legislatures provided funds in a way which left a large measure of control over policy to local school boards, and insisted on state control only in those areas where the public was of one mind: fire prevention, safe building codes, minimum requirements for teachers, etc. Where there was a conflict of assumptions in the public mind about the schools, where the ideas of cooperation and competition came into conflict, political representatives perhaps wisely stayed away. The citizen is always easily aroused by threats to his pocketbook. To become identified with controversial programs affecting his child as well is a risky business. Legislatures have only rarely proposed a specific curriculum, though there has been a disturbing tendency in recent years to explore this path. In many states a substantial portion of the money for the schools is raised by state appropriation, yet it is generally agreed that state control over curriculum has not yet followed the dollar.

On the other hand, the chief executive of city or town, whether large or small, would like to have an active voice in the control of the costs of the schools, for many of the members of the public hold him accountable for the tax rate. In most parts of the country, however, this power is assigned to the local school board, with substantial power to set the budget. The conflict of interest is clear. The specialist in political affairs points out that divided authority results in duplication and inefficiency. The educator argues that to put the schools under direct political administration is to endanger academic freedom, and to run the risk that the schools will be used to support the particular views of one party or one powerful individual. Against this, they feel every safeguard must be erected. The lay board, the professional staff, and the power of appropriation are the best guarantees.

The main point is that Americans are faced with a difference of opinion among those with concerns in the formation of educational policy. The Congress has consistently added to its legislation, obviously designed to affect the schools and colleges, the qualification that the federal government must not interfere in matters of personnel, curriculum, or management. Further, as earlier chapters have also indicated, different assumptions exist about what the schools should accomplish, not only differences between the individuals, but even differences within the same individual. There has been lack of agreement on the best procedure for settling the problems that arise as the result of these inevitable clashes.

Some observers of the American scene have been surprised that such areas of confusion and potential conflict have not created more serious operating difficulties than they have. Without clearly established purposes, and with a built-in conflict within the government structure, How does the machine work at all? they ask.

There seem to be two major answers. The first is a matter of social organization. The American people are accustomed to the confusions of a pluralistic scheme of things. Duplication is not feared; indeed it is often welcomed under the name of competition. There is a willingness to give the other man's assumptions a run for their money as long as they do not obviously interfere with the general welfare. In educational matters, there is a tendency to permit practices to develop as long as they do not, in the phrase made famous in the law by Justice Holmes, represent "a clear and present danger." The tent of education for all is generous and accommodating: all manner of ideas find comfort and shelter.

A second reason might be called an accident of history. The growth of new functions to be taken on by the schools; the development of more elaborate administrative structures in all aspects of government, including the schools; and the provision of a longer period for the process of education, all coincided in time. Only in the last fifty years, after all, have educational reform, the child labor laws, and other requirements made it possible for the great majority of children to attend school during their adolescent years. Proponents of new ideas about what should be taught were not, therefore, forced to make a case that their idea was so good that it should displace some existing program. They could rather urge that it be added to an expanding enterprise—which had room for still further additions. As long as this was true the conflicts of assumptions rarely came out in the open: the arguments fell more generally into the pattern of economic rather than political or philosophical analysis. Since most of the proposals for new responsibilities were, in addition, "good," in the sense that they could be seen to help at least some children, there was little disposition to accuse their proponents of evil intent. The result has been the variety of programs that characterizes the American secondary school. And the result has also been that the assumption by school boards and school administrators of functions of government planning has gone on largely unnoticed by the American people or their political leaders.

The future will not be as easy a road to travel as the past. How long can we afford (for psychological if not financial reasons) to extend the length of schooling? Can new ideas be absorbed in the future by adding to the curriculum without eliminating something already there? Will government continue to leave decisions in the hands of independent agencies strongly influenced by a professional group with special interests? Or will there be increasing pressure to relate the policy function of education to other decisions of government?

The answers are already written in the legislation of the middle 1960's: they will *have* to be related.

v The Capacity of the States and National Educational Policy

Educational needs can no longer be, if they ever could have been, considered apart from society's other needs—or from politics. Education may be as deeply affected by the Civil Rights Act of 1964, the income tax laws or the Appalachian Regional Development Act of 1965, as by the education bills of 1965 itself. Education is not a special need of a particular group in society. It is the business of everyone and affects everyone.

Walter Lippmann framed the challenge of the necessary revolution in this way: ". . . we must measure not by what it would be easy and convenient to do, but what it is necessary to do in order that the Nation may survive and flourish. We have learned that we are quite rich enough to defend ourselves, whatever the cost. We must now learn that we are quite rich enough to educate ourselves as we need to be educated."

President Johnson, in his message to Congress, argued that the goal of a Great Society cannot be considered apart from the society's educational system. And educational goals have to face these issues: (a) how best to fuse national interests with private, state, and local responsibility in providing both equality of opportunity and high quality of education; (b) how best to give proper weight to innovation and to the views of the scholars and other experts in the areas of knowledge that should be taught; and (c) how best to strengthen the machinery of government to relate educational policies and programs to other needs of the society.

The 88th and 89th Congresses wrote out in a series of new acts between 1963 and 1965 the national approach to these problems. These acts provided:

1. That the national interest in assuring equal opportunity for education is to be expressed by special programs for the economically, educationally, and physically disadvantaged—relying on local, state, and private funds for the management and funding of the regular budgets of schools and colleges. Programs are to be designed for the needy pupils, whatever their school, under public auspices—thereby setting a new pattern for local cooperation on the church-state issue.

2. That support of research, development, and innovation is a national responsibility, to be conducted by making grants designed to unite the interests of scholars and schoolmen in the creation of new and better curricula, and the discovery of better ways to prepare teachers and diffuse effective practices. Contracts with industry for research are authorized to tap the energy and skills of the private sector of the economy.

3. That decisions on operating programs in the schools supported by federal funds (as distinguished from the programs in 2, above) should be made by state authorities on the basis of local proposals. For this purpose federal funds should be made available to the states for support of personnel and procedures to strengthen state departments of education.

4. That it is in the national interest to expand facilities for higher education to meet the demands of the onrushing generations. The role of the federal government is also to finance through grants, loans, and work-study programs the costs of such education for worthy students in need, and to help to provide college faculty.

5. That a start should be made in assessing the results of these programs by requiring data from local and state authorities and by the establishment of advisory committees, several of which were directed to report to the President and the Congress.

6. That federal expenditures should be over and above, not in place of, existing expenditures.

These actions, when seen in the longer perspective, were but another turning of the wheel in the revolution that started nearly two

Table 12. Chronology of major education legislation passed by the 88th Congress and the first session of the 89th Congress

	Public law number	Title of law	Date signed by President
1.	88–129	Health Professions Educational Assistance Act of 1963	9/24/63
2.	88–164	Education Provisions (Title III), Mental Retardation Facilities and Community Mental Health Centers Construction Act of 1963	10/31/63
3.	88–204	Higher Education Facilities Act of 1963	12/16/63
4.	88–210	Vocational Education Act of 1963	12/18/63
5.	88–214	Manpower Development and Training Act, Amendments of 1963	12/19/63
6.	88–269	Library Services and Construction Act of 1964	2/11/64
7.	88–352	Civil Rights Act of 1964: Titles IV and VI	7/2/64
8.	88–368	Juvenile Delinquency and Youth Offenses Contract Act, Amendments of 1964	7/9/64
9.	88–452	Economic Opportunity Act of 1964	8/20/64
10.	88–579	National Arts and Cultural Development Act of 1964	9/3/64
11.	88–581	Nurse Training Act of 1964	9/4/64
12.	88–665	National Defense Education Act, Amendments of 1964; and School Assistance to Federally Affected Areas, Amendments of 1964	10/16/64
13.	89–10	Elementary and Secondary Education Act of 1965	4/11/65
14.	89–15	Manpower Development and Training Act, Amendments of 1965	4/26/65
15.	89–36	National Technical Institute for the Deaf Act	6/8/65
16.	89–69	Juvenile Delinquency and Youth Offenses Control Act, Amendments of 1965	7/8/65
17.	89–105	Training Teachers of the Handicapped, Amendments to P.L. 88–164	8/4/65
18.	89–209	National Foundation on the Arts and the Humanities Act of 1965	9/29/65
19.	89–253	Economic Opportunity Act, Amendments of 1965	10/9/65
20.	89–258	Captioned Films for the Deaf, Amendments of 1965	10/19/65
21.	89–287	National Vocational Student Loan Insurance Act of 1965	10/22/65
22.	89–290	Health Professions Educational Assistance Act, Amendments of 1965	10/22/65
23.	89–291	Medical Library Assistance Act of 1965	10/22/65
24.	89–313	Disaster Relief for Schools	11/1/65
25.	89–329	Higher Education Act of 1965	11/8/65

centuries ago. For the federal government has for many years compensated individuals for what they have given the nation or lost to it. Thus federal funds for education have gone to veterans and their children, who have given something to the nation; and to Indians on reservations, who have had something taken away.

The Congress has also made expenditures which it thought would be in the interest of the nation and its people as a whole. This second kind of federal grant dates back to the first days of our republic. The Preamble to the Ordinance of 1787, for example, declared that "an educated populace being to the benefit of society," one section of every township carved out of the vast Northwest Territory should be reserved, tax-free, for schools. Tax laws have long supported nonprofit educational enterprises.

The Smith-Hughes vocational legislation of 1917 stemmed at least partially from the nation's wartime shortage of skilled mechanics. The National Science Foundation was established after the Second World War to meet a gap in the national resources, just as the National Defense Education Act of 1958 won passage because threatening developments abroad convinced Congress that the nation needed more persons trained in science, mathematics, and in the neglected languages of Asia and Africa.

Both the earlier and the recent legislation provide federal support of education and cannot accurately be described as federal *aid* to education in the sense of direct support to ongoing programs. In some cases, such as the GI Bill, programs grew out of a national sense of indebtedness to certain individuals; the primary purpose was not to benefit education as such—that is, schools or colleges. Other kinds of federal support came about because America needed certain kinds of skilled persons; the schools and colleges that trained them were paid for services rendered. And the large amounts which the government spent in university-conducted research were another instance of payment of this kind. It is fair to say that until the mid-1960's schools and colleges received benefits from federal funds more as a by-product of aid to individuals or causes than by direct intent.

In no case has federal money been voted as *aid* in the usual sense of that word. The traditional thinking on federal expenditures in the national interest still prevails. Hence to speak of "federal aid" simply confuses the issue. It is more appropriate to speak of federal *support for* special purposes. It might be appropriate to think of federal funds —or, for that matter, state or local funds—as an *investment* in education, an investment made by a partner who has clearly in mind the investments of other partners—local, state, and private.

In the early 1960's the federal investment in the operation of the public elementary and secondary schools averaged no more than 4 percent, with all the rest of the support for this national enterprise coming from state and local sources. With the passage

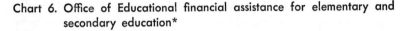

Chart 6. Office of Educational financial assistance for elementary and secondary education*

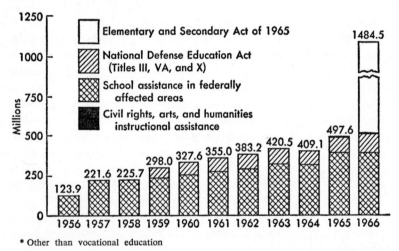

* Other than vocational education

SOURCE: Budget Office, Office of Education of the U.S. Department of Health, Education, and Welfare.

of the Elementary and Secondary Education Act it is estimated that the federal share will increase during the first year (1965–66) to nearly 8 percent. The percentage for higher education is more than double that for the schools. In neither area could the federal investment be described as the majority interest in the partnership, though it became clear that orchestration was needed among the varied programs of federal agencies that used schools and colleges to carry on their missions. The Congress, under the leadership of Congresswoman Edith Green of Oregon, pointed out the need. President Johnson established an interagency group to wrestle with the problem.

In voting for the Elementary and Secondary Education Act of 1965 many members of the Congress may have been thinking in terms of general support for schools or colleges but in fact voted in terms of investment—investment in people and therefore in the nation. As the record revealed, they supported the conservation of human resources and the opportunity for each American to make his appropriate contribution to the society and to share in its rewards. They may have thought also about the stimulating effect an improved educational structure would have on the rate of growth of the Gross National Product.

In effect, the federal government placed two restrictions on its investments: the first, which needed no explicit statement, was the normal expression of judicial restraint that federal funds could not be used for purposes declared unconstitutional by the United States Supreme Court; the second, that if federal funds were to be used at all, they must be used to improve the quantity and quality of education. In short, federal funds could legitimately be spent on education only if they served the interest of the nation at large, and only if the federal interest was additive. Within those general considerations,

Table 13. The importance of Title I funds (Elementary and Secondary Education Act) in state education budgets: selected states

Area	Children (ages 5–17) in families earning less than $2,000 annually or receiving welfare aid	percent of all children in area	percent of school budget paid by Title I 1965–66
U.S.A.	5,500,000	11.0	—
Mississippi	255,000	40.5	15.1 ($31,000,000)
California	309,000	8.3	2.3 (78,000,000)
New York	300,000	6.0	3.6 (110,000,000)
Maryland	63,000	7.0	2.8 (15,000,000)
Texas	398,000	16.0	6.4 (78,000,000)
Illinois	230,000	6.0	4.5 (61,000,000)

SOURCE: Office of Education, U.S. Department of Health, Education, and Welfare.

federal funds often were to be apportioned in ways that are in a sense "unequal," for they were to be given in response to special need.

Some states are, of course, poorer than others, and it was deemed to be in the interest of the nation as a whole that the children in those states not receive a correspondingly poorer education. Poor education inevitably reinforces the poverty of a state by diminishing the capacity of its people to produce, to earn, and to consume, by discouraging capital investment in that state, and by draining away talented young people who go elsewhere for college or better jobs, and seldom return. Hence, the formulas for distributing funds for the educationally disadvantaged gave greater benefit to the states with least ability to finance themselves.

The appropriation of substantial sums (see Table 14) suggested that the nation was, in Walter Lippmann's words, "rich enough to educate ourselves as we need to be educated." But was the educational machinery adequate to do the job?

Table 14. Elementary and Secondary Education Act of 1965: 1966 Appropriations

		Appropriation
Title I:	Education of Children of Low Income Families	$ 775,000,000
Title II:	School Library Resources and Instructional Materials	100,000,000
Title III:	Supplementary Educational Centers and Services	75,000,000
Title IV:	Educational Research and Training; Cooperative Research Act	45,000,000
Title V:	State Departments of Education	17,000,000
	Total	$1,012,000,000

SOURCE: Office of Education, U.S. Department of Health, Education, and Welfare.

Since the organizational unit that handles by far the largest number of students is the local school district, it deserves first attention. There are 27,000 school districts, each with some kind of lay board and each with a large measure of independence. Some, like New York City, are so large as to have raised doubts about whether they can be effectively managed. Others are so small that no reasonable man can argue their viability. All of them conduct their affairs in relation to fifty state departments of education (or public instruction, as they are sometimes called), varying in strength from powerful to pitiful, and over 2,600 institutions offering instruction above the high school level, again varying from the huge to the tiny, from the strong to the weak.

It has been argued that the glory of education in the United States has been its diversity. We have encouraged the kind of local initiative that is lacking, for example, in the French or in the Italian system. The advantage of diversity is the advantage of the diffusions of centers of initiative. The disadvantage is the difference in quality of education and the difficulty in adjustment faced by students who, in an increasingly mobile society, move from one place and one school to another.

The diffusion of centers of initiative in the United States has kept a fluid system alive, permitting the existence of some remarkably good institutions as well as some remarkably bad ones. The decentralized local educational system has allowed experimentation and variation, and the development of strong educational programs which have been described as lighthouses. Other districts, seeing the glow, have aspired to similar excellence. The dullness of mediocrity, which theoretically can result from more centralized systems, is thus avoided, according to those who plead for no change in present arrangements. The choice here is not between good and evil. Diversity and consistency or coherence (far different from conformity) are both good. But a range that admits of inferior standards is, in the national interest, unacceptable.

Diversity has left many districts unable economically to finance the exemplary programs even when they wished to. Too often the "lighthouse" districts have been primarily the result of concentrations of wealth into small districts with little effect on their neighbors. If there have been concentrations of wealth, there have also been concentrations of poverty.

If "equality of quality" in education is to have meaning, it necessarily applies to the poor as well as the rich, to the Negro as well as the white, to the bright as well as the average. It applies to every student without favor and without regard to the place in which he happens to live. There can be no inequality based on accidents of geography.

Again, let us look at the facts. The sections of the country with the lowest per capita income tend to have the heaviest educational burden. And within states, also, inequality is common. A child in a rural community or urban slum has less chance for a good education than a suburban child. Inequities exist from region to region, from state to state, from urban to rural, from slum to suburb. In 1960, 63 percent of college-age children of white-collar workers, 29 percent of manual and service workers' children, and 27 percent of farm workers' children went to college.

When one looks at a list of state average current expenditures per child for public elementary and secondary schools, which range from a low of $249 to a high of $746 (1963–64 data) and a low of $317 to a high of $876 (1965–66 estimates), it is clear that in no sense is the child from the state at the bottom receiving educational benefits comparable to those given the child at the top, if measured in dollars. The range of median expenditures between states for cost per classroom unit in 1959–60 was better than three to one (New York, $12,215; Arkansas, $3,645). The estimated average teachers' salaries in 1965–66 range from $4,190 in Mississippi and $4,650 in South Dakota to $7,700 in New York and $8,240 in Alaska. A beginning teacher in South Dakota may receive $2,700, one in California or New York $5,500 or more.

It is scarcely surprising then that the median years of school completed varies from region to region and from state to state. In 1960, the average person twenty-five years old and over had 9.6 years of school in the South, 10.7 years in the Northeast and North Central regions, and 12 years in the West. The range among states was from 8.7 years in South Carolina and Kentucky to 12.2 years in Utah.

It has been said that the migration from poor rural states to richer urban states has hurt both groups. This apparent paradox is based upon the assumption that the best-trained or most ambitious usually will make the move from adverse conditions. They often bring to their point of destination, however, an educational background below average for their new place of residence. The burden and impact of poor educational support is no longer confined to an individual state or region.

Yet it must be noted that the range of expenditures is greater for school districts *within* states than is the range of averages *between* states. In even the lowest-expenditure states, some school districts spend close to or above the national average, and in most states that spend the highest on the average some districts spend less than the national average. In New York State in 1962–63, with an average approved operating expenditure of approximately $680 per pupil, some school districts spent more than $2,000 per pupil, and others less than $300.

The wealthier, better-staffed school districts are the ones with the language laboratories, science equipment, planetariums, mathematics laboratories, greenhouses, integrated textbooks (but often little integration), testing services, public address systems, and the like. It is not only that educational leaders with more original ideas serve in the wealthier districts, or that the less imaginative serve in poor districts, but rather that the ability or lack of ability to buy is also a factor—for even salesmen and distributors steer clear of those districts with which they cannot "do business."

According to the poverty standard established at $3,000 net yearly income from the Economic Opportunity Act of 1964, nearly half of the poor in the United States live in rural areas in which the proportion of poverty-level families is almost twice as great as in the city. Among all persons who make up poor rural families, 6 million are children under eighteen years, and 1.2 million are sixteen to twenty-one years old. About three in every four members of poor rural families are white.

Rural schools, therefore, are inevitably often inferior in many respects, and a recent study of farm youth in the Midwestern, Southern, and Western states showed a lower elementary and secondary school attendance there than in the urban population. Only 55 percent of farm operators' children fifteen to twenty-one years old have completed eight grades of school. About 50 percent of all individuals in farm workers' families are less than eighteen years old, and about one-half of these lag behind other children of their age in school progress. Ten percent of this farm-labor group are migrant citizens. The 1964 Manpower report of the President estimated their number at 600,000 (including members of the family that traveled with them). More than half of these migrants are between fourteen and thirty-four, unskilled, and of Mexican-American or Negro ethnic origin. It was obvious that children of these families had difficulty keeping up in school because of their migratory way of life.

About 4.9 million, or more than half of the poor families in the United States, live, on the other hand, in metropolitan areas of 250,000 population or more. In urban areas, nonwhites with low incomes are more concentrated than whites. About half of all poor white families live in cities, as do 63 percent of all nonwhites. The problem of place clearly has affected minorities with special force. A higher dropout rate and a general lower educational level are characteristic of pockets of poverty. The lack of resources to combat poverty inevitably leads to lower ambitions.

The Elementary and Secondary Education Act of 1965 and the Economic Opportunity Act were designed to provide an answer to these grim statistics. Combined they represent a major effort to correct some of the worst conditions in the poorest sections of the country. If they are successful, the range between low and high may lessen. Yet the range of expenditures, from low to high, between states and within states, spread in the decade of the fifties, the forward thrust doubtless caused by increasing affluence. The nation must therefore watch carefully lest the combined local, state, and federal programs fail to provide the lifting power necessary to provide for the poorer districts a more rapid rate of progress.

Analysis of this issue leads into the complex problem of the methods of financing schools. Traditionally, states have provided an equal dollar amount per pupil—called the "foundation"—for all the school districts of the state. Local school districts were required to levy a given property tax rate for their share of the foundation amount. The difference between the foundation amount and the funds raised locally by the property tax rate has been provided by the state. As the spending per pupil has advanced in the past fifteen years, however, the foundation amount defined by state law has lagged behind. The foundation amount has become a smaller and smaller percentage of the average statewide per-pupil expenditure. At the same time, states have increasingly used percentage-of-cost grants, matching grants, and other stimulation grants which demand additional local funds. As a result of both of these trends, state grants

Chart 7. Government expenditures for education in 1962

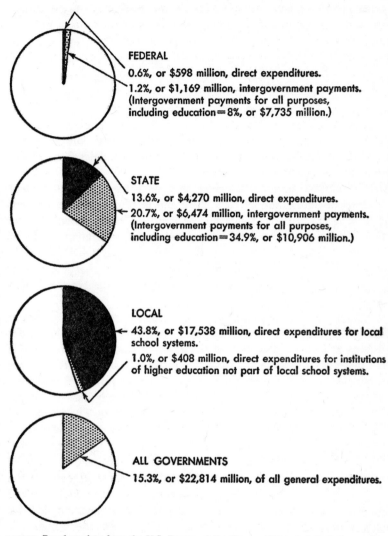

FEDERAL

0.6%, or $598 million, direct expenditures.

1.2%, or $1,169 million, intergovernment payments.
(Intergovernment payments for all purposes,
including education = 8%, or $7,735 million.)

STATE

13.6%, or $4,270 million, direct expenditures.

20.7%, or $6,474 million, intergovernment payments.
(Intergovernment payments for all purposes,
including education = 34.9%, or $10,906 million.)

LOCAL

43.8%, or $17,538 million, direct expenditures for local
school systems.

1.0%, or $408 million, direct expenditures for institutions
of higher education not part of local school systems.

ALL GOVERNMENTS

15.3%, or $22,814 million, of all general expenditures.

SOURCE: Based on data from the U.S. Bureau of the Census; "Historical Statistics on Government Finances," Census of Governments, Vol. 6, No. 4, November, 1964; chart
by the Office of Education.

Out of every dollar spent by federal, state, and local governments combined in 1962,
education took slightly more than 15 cents. But out of every dollar spent by local
governments, education took almost 45 cents, compared to 34 cents out of every dollar
spent by the states and less than 2 cents out of every dollar spent by the federal government.

no longer provide for a high degree of equalization but tend to provide proportionately more funds to wealthier school districts. Shifting population and property valuations have moved the great cities to about the middle of a distribution of school districts on property valuation per child in public schools. Both the suburban communities and rural communities with decreasing population now surpass the large cities. The suburban communities have gained relatively from the emphasis on percentage-of-cost grants and matching grants, for these school districts have had the necessary local funds. In the mid-1960's, the financing of education in the great cities has become America's most serious school problem.

Some limited progress has been made in recognizing the need of the cities in state grants in New York and in Illinois, where a recent grant program provides funds for the deprived urban schools. If the states recognize the need to make the foundation amount closer to per-pupil expenditure, including all districts in an equalizing formula for this amount, the lack of local funds will not be the deterrent to quality education that it now is in large cities of the Northeast and Midwest.

But inequality based on place is not a matter merely of a system that has worked out accidentally to the advantage of the wealthier suburbs and to the detriment of the cities. It seems safe to conclude that if the rural schools and the cities' public schools were the centers of education for the middle and upper class whites, as the suburbs are, they would be receiving more funds, better equipment, better-paid, better-educated, and more experienced teachers. The absence of the children of the majority—and of community leaders—from these urban schools has weakened their ability to act in their own behalf. The disadvantaged character of these schools cannot be demonstrated by financial statistics alone; it is revealed even more urgently in the statistics of inferior educational performance of their children and the social consequences of poor education—unemployment, low income, broken and dependent families, delinquency and crime.

These problems have traditionally been issues for state government to solve, but the federal government, in its actions of the mid-1960's, entered the scene with unparalleled vigor. It did so with certain restrictions, however, for it pronounced the policy that basic responsibility for management must remain with the states. It reaffirmed the policy that the structure of the American schools must rest on a strong state foundation. Title V of the Elementary and Secondary Act, which provides federal help to strengthen state departments of education, is evidence of the underlying belief that the states are the basic instruments in the management of America's system of elementary and secondary education. The importance of this decision cannot be overstated. For the nation in 1965 reached a new plateau of challenge. The social and economic changes placed a far higher order of demand and stress upon schools than ever before. Most of this stress was placed upon the educational leadership of the states and, in large measure, upon the state departments of education.

In the long run, therefore, nothing that the citizen or the educator can do, wherever he may be, can be more important than strengthening the capacity of the states to respond to the educational needs of our time. This is the crux of the challenge. In education, the nation looks to the states not merely as a matter of law or precedent, but as a matter of practical soundness and necessity. In a nation of fifty states operating vast and independent enterprises for education, the federal government decided to help, as a partner—but only as a partner.

Yet the present situation in the states is far from satisfactory. The inadequacy of methods of financing has been shown. If the national goal of equal educational opportunity is to be met, if the nation is to assure the strength—perhaps even the viability—of America's decentralized system of public education, state organization and state policies will need a thorough overhaul. To bring about this change requires action in three key requirements: the need for better information on the condition of education within the states and among the states; the need for stronger leadership and planning by state departments of education in relation to local districts; and the need for innovation based upon sound research throughout the educational enterprise. Innovation need not always be based on research. Some of it should be the fruit of genuine creativity, some of plain courage, some of ingenious artistry. Good research is, of course, to be encouraged and more of it is needed, but it is not in every case essential to school improvement.

In each of these problem areas, the federal government decided to help—and was called upon to help—in providing both perspective and funds. But the strategic link between America's 27,000 autonomous school districts and Washington is within the states—and it is here that American education may ultimately meet or fail to meet the extraordinary imperatives of our time.

Chart 8. Office of Education total appropriations

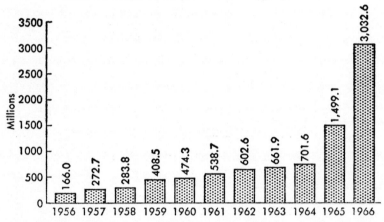

SOURCE: Budget Office, Office of Education of the U.S. Department of Health, Education, and Welfare.

Consider, for example, the problem of organization of school districts—the kind of complicated issue in modern society on which so much turns if change is to take place, if quality of education is to be improved.

The very disparities in financing among school districts clearly suggest that much needs to be done. One way to improve the situation, long recognized by educators, is to consolidate school districts. This has been happening to a growing extent, especially as improved highways made bus transportation more feasible. About 50,000 one-teacher schools have been closed in the United States since 1950; and since 1950 some 57,000 school districts have been combined with others, leaving a total today of about 27,000.

The school-consolidation movement in rural areas grew out of the inability of small schools to offer a full range of programs. Something much better than the typical country school was needed if farm youth was to get even a reasonably varied high school education; larger schools were necessary for broadening elementary curricula, for improving the quality of instruction, and for attracting and keeping capable teachers. The goal was presumably to improve education, not to reduce school taxes; yet consolidated schools did in fact yield more and better education per school-tax dollar. Perhaps the most striking result of the consolidation movement was the near elimination of the one-teacher school as an important part of rural school organization.

Yet the picture varies widely from state to state. While Hawaii has only one district, Nevada seventeen, and Maryland twenty-four districts, Nebraska and South Dakota have between 2,000 and 3,000 each. As recently as 1962, four-fifths of all operating districts contained fewer than 1,200 pupils.

Consolidation of small high schools has been much more complex. Most small high schools were village-centered and thus already represented consolidations of a sort. Soon after their establishment years ago, many began taking in tuition-paying pupils from surrounding open-country districts. Some areas created separate high school districts. In either case, the result was essentially the same: each village, large or small, got its own high school, developed pride in it, and resisted any attempt to change its organizational status.

With the passage of time, many of these organizational arrangements, especially in smaller villages, progressively deteriorated. Population migration resulted in declining enrollments, smaller classes, poorer use of staff, and ever higher per-pupil costs year after year. In such schools it has become almost impossible to provide the expanding array of courses and instructional services needed in a modern program. This was the situation which led Conant to say (in *The American High School Today*) that district consolidation was the basic and drastic change necessary for improving high school programs.

Ironically, at the same time that many rural communities are struggling toward equality and solvency by establishing bigger districts and bigger schools, the great city school systems are trying to overcome the disadvantages that bigness can produce. A number of the cities, including New York, Chicago, Los Angeles, Detroit, Philadelphia, St. Louis, and Atlanta, have started to decentralize their administrative organization by dividing into subdistricts. The sheer force of numbers will doubtless force the city systems to decentralize still further and one may hope that decentralization will include such variations as a model school subsystem.

Other techniques are being considered, including experimental programs to consolidate clusters of urban schools into educational parks, and plans to decentralize school administrative jurisdiction. The trend toward consolidation through educational parks stems from much the some motivation felt in rural communities: the desire to eliminate duplication of services, to provide modern equipment, and to hire better teachers, plus the determination to counteract *de facto,* residence-controlled segregation by establishing clusters of quality schools in the city.

School consolidation in rural areas and school system decentralization in large cities, although apparently headed in opposite directions, in fact share the same purpose of removing handicaps imposed by size, to the end of providing better educational opportunities. These were the purposes also of the new federal initiative in education in the mid-1960's. But on the issue of organization and administration, Congress was silent, as it was on issues of personnel appointments, decisions on curriculum or housing, and other aspects of the management of schools. Such issues should be handled by leadership from the state, not the federal, government. Again and again the Congress adopted language to make clear its wish that the federal executive branch should not "control" American education:

FEDERAL CONTROL OF EDUCATION PROHIBITED

SEC. 604. Nothing contained in this Act shall be construed to authorize any department, agency, officer, or employee of the United States to exercise any direction, supervision, or control over the curriculum, program of instruction, administration, or personnel of any educational institution or school system, or over the selection of library resources, textbooks, or other printed or published instructional materials by any educational institution or school system.

The federal government, then, is to participate as a partner with special interests in the educational affairs of the nation. On the issues of local management it proposes to provide the facilities for research and development, the support of innovative ideas, the encouragement of national perspective—but not legislative direction or administrative oversight. Nationwide problems were identified and programs adopted to help schools and colleges to solve them: disadvantaged children, shortage of trained teachers, discrimination, lack of innovation, and many others. The mid-1960's saw the terms of a new federal, state, and local partnership being worked out in education as they had been in other aspects of the national life before. Federal control in any direct sense on any school or college was barred, but federal influence toward national goals was established. Checks and balances between federal, state, and local spheres of influence were outlined and a start made on finding ways to work toward common goals. The task was far from easy, for a long tradition of suspicion of the danger of federal control was widespread in both lay and professional thinking. Bureaucracy is always a matter of concern; the danger of a national bureaucracy imposing its will on school children was enough to demand special measures to assure that federal initiative should not become federal imposition.

The first measure adopted was the requirement in bill after bill of advisory committees on policies and procedures. Such groups often also served as independent sources for the reporting of results to the President and the Congress. They were usually made up of men and women who were not government employees. Though not written into legislation, a second check against improper federal action lay in the powers of voluntary educational associations, often with Washington offices in close touch with Congress, which could keep watch on the interests of their membership. Perhaps most important of all, the President and the Congress joined in efforts to strengthen the quality of the state departments for education by special grants of funds in Title V of the Elementary and Secondary Education Act, and by the statutory requirement that these departments take the responsibility for educational decisions on programs financed from federal sources. There were many who doubted the capacity of the states to do the job. Some local districts feared too much state power.

Large-city schools showed signs of wanting to do business directly with Washington rather than through the state capitol, though the Supreme Court ruling on equal apportionment promised to give the cities a better chance in the state legislatures of the future.

The decision to work out a new federal, state, and local partnership, with checks against the danger of undue power in the hands of any one authority, was a characteristic American solution to the problem. The federal system, established after one revolution, needs constant revision and adaptation to meet new needs.

For the federal role could not be passive. Its activities had to take into account social facts that distinguished one part of the country from another. It had to recognize, for example, the movement of the population, and differences in economic abilities. By methods by which the large programs for the education of the disadvantaged were financed in the Elementary and Secondary Education Act of 1965, the differences in wealth among the states were partly redressed. A special program for small colleges that suffered from lack of financial means and adequate faculty was established in the Higher Education

Table 15. Higher Education Act of 1965: 1966 Appropriations

		Appropriation
Title I:	University Extension and Continuing Education	$ 10,000,000
Title II:	College Library Assistance and Library Training and Research	—
Title III:	Strengthening Developing Institutions	5,000,000
Title IV:	Student Assistance	
	A. Undergraduate Scholarships	60,000,000
	B. Insured, Reduced-Interest Loans	10,000,000
	C. College Work-Study Program Extension and Amendments	40,000,000
	(Additional $59,123,000 in Economic Opportunity Act)	
Title V:	Teacher Programs	20,000,000
Title VI:	Financial Assistance for Improvement of Undergraduate Instruction	15,000,000
	Total	$160,000,000

SOURCE: Budget Office, Office of Education of U.S. Department of Health, Education, and Welfare.

Act of the same year. College students without means were supported through loans, grants, and the subsidized opportunity to earn part of their way through colleges. By these and other means federal activities linked the country together and played an active role, with its state, local, and private partners, in moving toward the goal of equality of educational opportunity.

At the same time movements toward local and regional cooperation intensified. New York State, for example, developed regional arrangements to provide special educational services to the school districts in the geographical area. With the aid of grants from Title V of the Elementary and Secondary Education Act, several states combined to undertake joint studies and activities on a regional basis. And an interstate compact was organized with the backing of a number of governors and legislatures to study issues of common interest. As the federal interest in education became more clearly expressed, local and state authorities have re-formed their relationships to adjust to the new situation. Countervailing powers are being created to assure protection against misuse of power from any one source. A new and creative federalism is in the making in education.

VI Quality in Education: The Teachers*

Most Americans have been ambivalent on education: they inherit and admire the aristocratic standards of the past and yet believe in twentieth-century democracy. But intellectual aristocracy and democracy need not be at odds. American democracy can afford and needs to be excellent as well as equal. Both quality and quantity are possible as far as dollars are concerned. The American people can afford both if they insist upon it, as they have increasingly come to do. The nation is clearly no longer content with mediocrity, with just "getting by." It is demanding excellent education for all. Quality education has come to imply integration, for a white child taught in isolation is a deprived child. It implies an end to the double standard in education, a double standard that gives high-quality schooling to students in exclusive suburbs and inferior schooling to children in slums, that gives preference to some states over others.

The quality of an educational program is to be measured by the product of three variables: the intent, the students and teachers, and the setting. To compare two schools means more, therefore, than to compare two buildings or two sets of examination records, or two statements of educational aims. A marked difference in any one of the three variables will affect the sum that we call quality.

A great deal of the confusion about American education today

* Some of the material in this chapter was developed earlier in somewhat different form in the 1961 Horace Mann Lecture, "Personnel Policies for Public Education." Copyright © 1961 by University of Pittsburgh Press. Reprinted by permission.

springs from the fact that we do not make it clear which variable has caught our interest at the time we speak. It is perfectly possible for someone who is interested in educational purpose to be rebutted by someone who thinks largely of social setting and equality of opportunity. But perhaps "rebutted" is the wrong term. There is often no real conflict of statement, no real "butting" of ideas. Such discussions add little to the solution of the concrete problems that face the schools in troubled times.

A comparable situation seems to exist in talking about quality, particularly when considered in the light of needs for quantity. A distinguished literary scholar, Professor Douglas Bush, reached the gloomy conclusion that the two were incompatible. *The New York Times Magazine* once headlined an article he wrote: "Education for All Is Education for None." To this statement the advocates of widespread public education responded with some heat. They pointed out that the general level of literacy rose in a half-century, that students of widely varied ability were now cared for in schools, and that the varied social settings of schools in many cases made a common standard of educational performance impossible and unwise.

Some argue that quantity and quality are by their very nature incompatible, and that current educational arrangements have resulted in too low a level of intellectual standards and general esthetic taste both for those with an academic cast of mind and for the general public. This argument tends to assume that social setting or abilities of students or teachers are relevant but less important, and that the standard performance in academic disciplines marks a civilized society. Those who disagree point to the need to give an equal chance to all, to the adjustment of youth to an age of technology, to the fact that an ever-higher percentage of youth is entering college. They tend to feel, if not to say, that academic standards will take care of themselves.

It is possible to be dissatisfied with both these positions. American education cannot be judged alone against a particular standard of academic excellence, important though this is. The schools are a part of a mobile society and they are and will be used to solve social problems as well. There seems to be no reason to assume that American education cannot have both quality *and* quantity at the same time.

There is no logical conflict here, rather a difference in focus. The issue comes not in theory, it comes in the cold decision of what we can afford to do as a people, and what we think is important.

No factor in education, of course, influences the quality of learning the children receive more directly and forcibly than teachers. Superior teaching is the first requisite of providing an efficient educational program of good quality, for the teacher, while not all of education, is nevertheless most of it. Any discussion of methods to improve present-day educational practice must consider the education of teachers themselves.

Today, there are in the United States more than 2,200 institutions of higher education. Approximately 1,250 of these prepare elementary and secondary teachers. One-third of the new teachers in September are likely to be graduates of colleges or schools of education in approximately 160 universities. Another third will come from about 190 institutions which are largely teacher-preparatory, and the last third will come from some 900 liberal arts and general colleges which have departments of education.

Discussions of teacher education generally focus upon instruction and programs of courses, so that the relative importance of *training versus selection* is frequently not considered. Long and sometimes frustrating experience has suggested to many educators that selection is as important as training in teacher education. If a person with the basic qualifications for being a good teacher is attracted into education, it matters less which courses he takes; he will probably wind up a good teacher if he has had practice under guidance of a wise leader. On the other hand, a person without these basic qualifications will rarely be turned into a good teacher, no matter how enlightened the curriculum to which he is subjected or how progressive the faculty to which he is exposed.

There has been an uneasy relation between the universities and the schools in the recruitment and preparation of teachers partly because elementary schooling was not thought to be a suitable university concern. Recent years have brought a change in atmosphere as the findings and the speculations of the psychologists and the scientists have suggested that the mind of the young may be a new frontier. But for many years the universities by their intellectual snobbism about the study of education—which was not hard to understand because some professors of education wrote appalling nonsense—were missing the importance of the public schools as an instrument in the American society. This lack of understanding in the intellectual community resulted in a derogation of the institutions of elementary and secondary education by political scientists, historians, philosophers, and intellectuals in general. The colleges and schools of education, public or private, were said to be pretty dull places. The abler and more energetic undergraduates heard such accounts from their professors or from the young graduate students. In the face of such a reputation, for a man of ability to apply for admission to a school of education took moral courage. The result was also that competent, scholarly investigation was rarely applied to an important aspect of public life, and there was little encouragement for the coming generation of scholars or administrators to consider as a possible career one in the schools. An engine of the democracy, of great importance in a mobile society, was largely neglected by far too many of those most competent to study its needs and insufficiently staffed by those most capable of its leadership. The first task on any agenda to redesign teacher education has been to attract promising young people to the schools for a career. The nation has begun to reverse the inadequate policies of the past trend, but the pace must be speeded up. Where should the schools look for their personnel? What kind of training program is needed? What sort of personnel policies will attract and keep the educator of the future?

One of the first questions is whether or not a college education is necessary for every teacher in the schools. No wise man will seek entrance to heaven on the argument that it has been absolutely necessary in the past for a man or woman to graduate from a four-year college in order to teach the third grade, though the educational profession has sometimes made it sound that way. With the new curricula that seem to be ahead of us, however, college education becomes more necessary. The old argument for requiring a college education for elementary school teachers was, at least in part, the result of the need for some easily measured and readily accepted standard for appointment. The new argument must be based on the need for a subtler measure of quality: the ability to handle new ideas and new techniques.

Unfortunately, most programs of teacher education have tended to discourage many young men and women of the caliber needed. The reputation which the study of education and "teaching" courses enjoyed was far from favorable. But it was not only the reputation but the fact on which it was based that had to be changed. Fortunately, universities and colleges by the mid-1960's had begun to do so. But their efforts were impeded by the widespread (and all too often correct) conviction that no one in education could earn a decent living. In good school systems, initial salaries were reasonably competitive with opening salaries in many professions. The problem was the future. For young students the issue is not the bottom salary; it is the top salary. Where can they go? What kind of reasonable expectation of advancement may they have? What is the ceiling in teaching to the natural ambition of an able and vigorous college student or graduate?

In the answer to this last question lies part of the answer to both the problem of staffing the schools with a strong proportion of the most promising men and women of each generation and the problem of how best to use their talents.

Society now tells a young man who is thinking of teaching as a career that he can look forward only to a low ceiling in salary and responsibility. It says in effect that, if he starts teaching at twenty-one and remains a teacher, by retirement at the age of sixty-five, he will still influence the lives of only the same number of pupils in his classroom at any given time as when he began. They may well be the same age group. It must further report that ordinarily his salary will increase only to the extent that it reflects length of service and so many "hours" of graduate study. While young people heard rumors of some teachers' salaries above $10,000 per year in the 1960's, honesty compelled the report that they were few and far between. A cynic remarked that the fairest comparison of personnel policies of the public schools was to the old Army, in which one could tell the income of the soldier by looking at the sleeves of his uniform: On one were bars showing the number of re-enlistments, each of which brought a raise in pay. On the other were bars representing overseas service, and sometimes wound stripes. Similarly one could estimate the salary of teachers by their years of service and by their departure for further study—sometimes painful—in order to raise their position on the salary scale.

Obviously this was not a personnel policy exciting to the energetic young man or woman. The low salary ceiling was bad enough—but perhaps even worse was the lack of advancement, the lack of sense of career, and the absence of that increased responsibility which usually accompanies merit and experience. Business and law, government and industry, even higher education with its system of professorial ranks, offer such future possibilities. But not the schools!

To be sure, most teachers work at their profession fewer months of the year than the other professionals. Even so, the figures in Table 16 show a serious disparity between the earnings of teachers and those in the other occupations, for the teacher-earnings figure includes extra income from moonlighting and summer jobs. These extra earnings often come from nonprofessional employment at relatively low salary or rates.

Teacher salaries go up for about ten or fifteen years after they start. After ten to fifteen years the increases have tended to come to a halt in most systems. The systems have often been able to retain men teachers only because they promoted themselves by moving from one school system to another where the salary scales were higher. The range of salaries *between* systems has given the individual the freedom to advance his own career, but not adequately *within* a single system.

Very often, however, the young college student either has given up the thought of teaching as a career or has planned as soon as possible to become an administrator. Here the picture was far more appealing. A large number of responsible posts as principal or superintendent are always available. Salaries have risen since the Second World War. As administrators the ablest young men—and, one may hope, young women—can reasonably expect by the age of forty to earn salaries that compare favorably with the average of the income of many other professions. Top salaries, of course, do not compete with the top salaries in law or medicine or business. But they do compete with government service, with the average of most

Table 16. Median earnings of males with four or more years of college, in the experienced civilian labor force, with earnings in 1959, by selected occupation, age, and color: Unied States, 1960

Occupation	White			Nonwhite		
	25 to 34	35 to 44	45 to 54	25 to 34	35 to 44	45 to 54
Total experienced civilian labor force	$ 6,356	$ 8,797	$ 9,233	$4,439	$5,479	$5,482
Professional, technical, and kindred workers	6,316	8,818	9,346	4,524	5,872	5,934
Accountants and auditors	6,312	8,320	8,892	—	—	—
Clergymen	3,995	4,733	4,694	—	—	—
College professors and instructors	5,582	8,312	9,085	—	—	—
Dentists	10,810	15,241	13,597	—	—	—
Designers and draftsmen	5,977	7,840	8,023	—	—	—
Mechanical engineers	8,104	9,717	10,946	—	—	—
Lawyers and judges	7,296	12,187	14,210	—	—	—
Natural scientists	7,220	9,024	9,526	—	7,751	—
Biological scientists	5,515	8,026	8,557	—	—	—
Chemists	7,077	8,740	9,176	—	—	—
Mathematicians	8,153	—	—	—	—	—
Physicians and surgeons	5,013	19,877	21,204	2,958	—	—
Social scientists	6,946	9,335	9,928	—	—	—
Economists	7,115	10,902	10,785	—	—	—
Psychologists	6,828	8,975	—	—	—	—
Elementary teachers	5,136	6,037	6,359	4,145	4,855	—
Secondary teachers	5,252	6,636	7,154	3,944	4,756	5,611

SOURCE: U.S. Bureau of the Census. *U.S. Census of Population: 1960. Subject Reports. Occupation by Earnings and Education.* Final Report PC(2)–7B.

professions, surpass the majority of salaries in higher education, and represent a more than adequate standard of living.

Yet by emphasizing this administrative path to advancement alone, the nation runs the danger of neglecting the core of American education: the teaching staff in direct touch with the pupils. Is there a way out of this dilemma? Salaries, of course, should be increased. But this alone will not solve the problem of a general, national shortage of skilled personnel. The nation also faces the fact that the personnel structure of the schools is ill designed to attract or to hold anything like an adequate proportion of the nation's most skilled and promising young men and women. This is true above all when other professions are in need of the very same group.

There are some who believe that the shortage of good teachers is caused less by lack of promotion than by what they regard as the ridiculous "certification" requirements of the states, which keep out of teaching anyone who has not studied in certain prescribed courses, usually in "education." Every detached observer will agree that some of these requirements are needlessly complicated, and many will say that some of them could be eliminated. Undoubtedly these requirements, which by 1965 were undergoing vigorous reappraisal in many states, kept out some promising aspirants to a teacher's career.

Certification of teachers depends largely upon the common currency in the academic world: counting course credits on official transcripts. Conant made a notable contribution in urging that certification be based in good part upon demonstrated competence as a student teacher, for of course the final test of a teacher's education is his ability in the classroom. Again, as with changes in teacher training, the movement of reform was under way by the mid-1960's, led by the educators themselves. The need was to speed it up, and to relate changes in requirement and preparation to the level of demand in the years ahead.

The demand for new public school teachers (including those returning to the profession) was 895,000 for the period from the fall of 1960 through the fall of 1964. This demand was expected to rise to 996,000 for 1965–69, and to 981,000 for 1970–74. The largest number were expected to be required for replacement, accounting for more than 75 percent of the total demand.

Private schools had positions for 93,000 new teachers in the period from the fall of 1960 through the fall of 1964. A demand for 164,000 new teachers during the following ten years was estimated, with replacement accounting for about 60 percent.

Additions to faculty and professional staffs in colleges and universities were expected also to rise sharply in and after the 1960's. From 1960 to 1965, the demand for new full-time faculty and staff was 223,000. Projections indicated that this figure could increase to 302,000 during 1965–70 and to 308,000 from 1970–75.

The decades of the 1960's and 1970's, therefore, are a testing ground of recruitment, training, salary, and personnel policies of the schools. Can they adjust to the demand for very large numbers of new staff? Not only do new personnel have to be recruited, but those with a career in teaching in mind must be kept on the job. And better use has also to be made of part-time and short-term personnel. The question is not only how to improve present arrangements so that a brighter future can be held before the young career teacher, but also how to handle realistically the large number of teachers who stay on the job barely long enough to become valuable to the schools they serve. The solution lies not alone in the general raising of salaries for all teachers, including those who will stay only a few short years in the classroom; it is also a selective matter. The public understandably wishes to reward those who both stay in teaching and show special skills. The schools need a way of reordering their affairs so that those who have the qualifications and stay in the profession advance to positions of greater responsibility, positions which call for their influence to be extended to a larger number of students and which bring rewards of prestige and salary. For not only are salaries too low—they also do not offer enough range. It is assumed that all teachers are the same, and all teaching jobs alike. Common sense, of course, denies the former; the present situation does not deny the latter. A widening of the range calls for a change in the structure.

One suggestion seemed to show promise, though the results are far from complete. This was based on plans to reorganize schools by establishing *teams* of teaching personnel, including a leader, perhaps certain subject specialists, and a staff on junior status, encompassing teachers, interns, and aides. The leaders of such teams could be in direct relationship with the pupils, could handle many aspects of parental relations, and could give close supervision to the work of the junior members, many of whom would teach for only a few years. They would be directly responsible for the quality of the work done in their division of the school's work, and could be expected not only to supervise the inexperienced teachers or teacher's aides but also to play a major part in the pupils' lives by teaching in the classrooms for which they are themselves responsible. Such leaders, and their associates with specialized qualifications, could properly be put on a substantially higher salary scale than the junior teachers, whose duties would probably be largely restricted to a smaller number of pupils and to lesser responsibilities. The teams and their leaders would have different responsibilities at the several levels of school work—elementary, junior high, and high school. In the last case, for example, the leader would be, in effect, a new type of chairman for a subject area. The young teachers, who started in junior status, could aspire to leader status in due course. A possible career could be held before young people as an impetus to advancement and to making education their life work.

Team teaching is essentially, therefore, a method of staff deployment to provide the strongest possible program of education for children with the strongest personnel available. The term was coined in 1957; the movement started in the Franklin School of Lexington, Massachusetts, with the help and stimulation of the Harvard Graduate School of Education, to mean the use of a group of teachers—including specialists in reading and in science, for example, in an elementary school—"captained" by a leader, all teaching a particular group of children. The spread of the movement was rapid—probably too rapid—and came to mean any collaboration between teachers at any level. The early years were therefore characterized by superficiality of approach both as to personnel and to curricular policies. By the mid-1960's it was hard to estimate whether team teaching would become a more stable educational device. Relatively little had been done on a scale that could test the assumption that a new personnel structure could help to solve problems of recruitment. The idea of team teaching had much to contribute to American schools and unquestionably could lead to needed improvements in curricula and teacher preparation as well. Its potential, it was clear, was enhanced when coupled with other innovations; its value diminished when it became the only change introduced.

Four implications of the personnel reorganization suggested by team teaching deserve special comment. The first is that it would cost *more* than prior arrangements. But the funds could be distributed in a way which would reward ability, commitment, and willingness to take responsibility, and might therefore be expected to attract able and energetic young men and women into teaching as a career. The public may not always be willing to raise the salaries of *all* teachers in order to attract and hold a minority of the dedicated and skilled. But it may be willing to spend more money on a plan which gives promise of achieving this end by a program which keeps to minimum standards and raises and which rewards top qualifications.

Second is the implication that the "junior" teacher is no longer wholly responsible for what takes place in his or her classroom. The children would have to deal with several personalities during the course of the day, and recognize a hierarchy of responsibility. If these are disadvantages, which is subject to debate, the advantage of close supervision over inexperienced teachers is a counterbalance. The director of such a team would, in effect, be the clinical teacher of an in-service program of training—an arrangement long familiar in medical education.

Third, it is probable that the position of director of these teams or of specialist staff might attract *both* men and women. To provide continuity of policy and maintenance of standards, a core staff of career educators is always needed. The chances of keeping a higher proportion of young men in a lifetime career are ordinarily better than in the case of the young women. Some of the disadvantages of the single-salary schedule for equal work, so widely and wisely adopted, could be removed as men go up the ladder of greater responsibility and therefore greater salary for different types of work.

Finally, such a pattern of teams might bring the personnel structure of the schools into better alignment with the lessons learned in business, government, and the military. Here it has long been considered that too large a span of control is unwise. A leader, it is argued, can deal effectively with only a small number of people reporting directly to him—usually fewer than a dozen—in those aspects of human activity which require skilled and complex work and intimate personal relations. It has not been uncommon in American schools, however, for a school principal, with a host of noneducational problems on his desk, to be responsible for the teaching skills of more than a dozen teachers, to say nothing of other personnel reporting to him. Supervisors and superintendents are in a comparable situation. To put it bluntly, teachers in American classrooms have received appallingly little direction or supervision. The ancient and honorable tradition of each teacher as king in his classroom may have to give way in the days of the necessary revolution. The advantages of freedom to teach can be maintained by wise leaders, who can at the same time by their own teaching and supervision assure ever-higher quality of performance. If it has been heresy to question the king in his classroom, the coming revolution may call out for the heretics.

Such a personnel reorganization is quite a different matter from increasing the salary of teachers on the basis of "merit" alone. Courageous efforts to introduce plans of such merit increases have been made. The record is not a happy one. There were probably two reasons: there is no general agreement on what "good" teaching means; and, except for a few individuals of outstanding general reputation, and a few of quite the opposite, there is no way of making fine distinctions between teachers in neighboring classrooms. The product of education cannot be judged by piecework methods. And the decentralization of American schools, combined with their close tie to the opinion of the local community, means that irrelevant influences may enter to sway educational judgments. Efforts toward a merit system have tended to fail unless the linking of salary to responsibility was taken into account. To borrow from the sociologist's terms, what was needed was a change of *role*—a change of position from lesser to greater responsibility in the school, to which higher salary could be assigned.

In 1960, more than three-quarters of elementary schools throughout the nation were using the one-teacher-per-classroom type of instructional organization. The remaining minority of schools were organized according to a variety of plans that permitted some degree of departmentalization, so that some teachers whose special skill was science, for example, would move from classroom to classroom during the day to give students at various grade levels the benefit of special expertise.

The advantages of such a system were self-evident. Aside from the stimulation that specialist teaching offered the student, the departmentalized arrangement gave the teacher a chance to concentrate on the subject and keep up with new developments, rather than to dissipate professional energies by attempting to learn about new concepts in every subject in the curriculum.

Yet one must note that the advantages of departmentalization at the elementary level were by no means proven. Research provided no consistent evidence that children as a group learn more mathematics from a specialist than from a generalist, though there was some indication that able learners profit more from a specialist than do the average or slow students. Far more research and trial was needed before the educator could give a firm judgment to the public on the best system of personal organization.

Yet there was enough promise in the idea of combined teaching teams and special expertise so that the Congress in 1965, as a part of the President's education program, established a national Teacher Corps and encouraged emphasis on the establishment of master teachers and teaching teams. Through support of teacher-training programs emphasizing the school subjects, funded by the National Science Foundation and the Office of Education, the federal government starting in the 1950's had clearly stated its concern that teachers should be expert in their special subject. The emphasis at first was on the high school level, but a broadening to include the elementary school began to take place in the middle of the next decade.

It remains to be seen whether the continued impact of the Teacher Corps and the institutes for teachers, when added to the experiments going on in the schools themselves, will profoundly change the personnel and salary structure of American education.

Comparable efforts were also taking place in reorganizing students for better learning. The most dramatic was the modification of the grade structure in elementary schools. The program was designed to permit a child to pursue each field of learning at his own speed. Most learners find that they do better in some subjects than in others, that they pick up mathematics, for example, more readily than history or English. The normally graded school, it was argued, does not reflect this difference between individuals. A third-grade child learns third-grade arithmetic, third-grade reading, and so on, no matter whether he can go faster than his peers in a particular subject.

"The nongraded plan is a system of organization and nothing more," Goodlad and Anderson* report. In a more detailed sense, nongrading is a form of "vertical" organization of school—a means by which children move in at the lowest level, progress upward, and eventually leave from the top, upon the completion of the allotted span of years. The choice is strict; a school can only be "graded" or "nongraded." Through a plan of continuous progress, each child, under a program of individualized instruction, moves along the sequential steps of the learning process, not subject to chronological checkpoints (grades or years). This achievement is to be measured against his own ability and development rather than against the normative standard of a "graded expectancy." Some indeed have favored the phrase "continuous progress" as a more accurate description of the concept than "nongradedness."

Others point out that there is nothing very new about nongradedness, that it is a throwback to some of the virtues of the one-room rural school, in which the teacher truly dealt with a nongraded class. In modern times the movement dates from the creation of the nongraded primary unit in Milwaukee in 1942 and a subsequent development in Appleton, Wisconsin, a few years later. The current drive was given impetus by publication of the Goodlad-Anderson book in 1959. Since that time the spread has been rapid, even dramatic. It is probably the fastest-moving innovation on the American elementary school scene. For the most part it has been concentrated in the primary grades, with few schools attempting it at any higher grade levels. The focusing of attention on the schools of both urban slums and rural communities and the passages of the Elementary and Secondary Education Act of 1965 brought further attention to its advantages. When the schools of Prince Edward County, Virginia, were reopened in 1963, for example, nongradedness was introduced to meet the needs of pupils who had been deprived of any education for several years as a result of civil rights disputes. Its very flexibility commended it to those facing new problems.

Appraisals of the method ranged from ecstatic to dubious in the early 1960's, with a preponderance of approval. It seemed to restore

* J. I. Goodland and R. H. Anderson, *The Nongraded Elementary School,* New York: Harcourt, Brace and World, 1963.

a realism to school administration by facing the facts of individual differences and making it possible for educational programs to become flexible and responsive to the facts of the human situation. Yet by itself, like reform of teacher recruitment, or the reorganization of personnel or salary policies, reorganization of pupils could not alone be the road to achieving the quality of education needed by a changing society.

The type of preparation provided for the future teacher was also a major factor. For decades the nation heard a debate between the scholars and the professional educators on the matter. The former had grave doubts about the value of courses in education, which they felt to be largely without intellectual content. The latter felt that the scholars had little idea about the realities of teaching young children and adolescents. Both were partly right. Conant in the late 1930's proposed a truce in a speech at Columbia Teachers College, and established a new program at Harvard for the master's degree for future high school teachers which required the collaboration of the professors of the arts and science and the professors of education. Known as a Master of Arts in Teaching, it spread to other universities in the 1950's and gave promise of becoming the trend of the future in requiring simultaneous study in the student's academic subject, in the bases of educational policy, and in learning how to teach by doing it under supervised practice.

Emphasis on knowledge of the subject to be taught was further emphasized in the late 1950's by the demands to reform after the Russian Sputnik shed light on America's educational weaknesses. The National Science Foundation provided funds for special institutes for teachers of mathematics and the sciences and required that the program be in the subjects, not in the professional education courses. The Congress expanded the national interest in later years to include languages, history, geography, and other school subjects, and provided the U.S. Office of Education with substantial funds to finance still further teacher institutes. Indeed the pendulum swung so sharply toward federal emphasis on knowledge of subject matter by the teachers that the educational profession became gravely concerned that the real problems of instruction were being neglected by default.

The civil rights movement has helped to redress the balance. For it became clear that more was needed by the teachers of educationally disadvantaged and minority group children than knowledge of subject alone. Institutes for teachers were established in the mid-1960's to focus attention on the issues involved and on the best ways of teaching such pupils. Research investigations have been undertaken, and some consideration given to more sensitive and flexible teaching materials. New emphasis has been placed on the psychological orientation of teachers, on the motivation to teach. The needs of those whom the society had neglected therefore are helping to bring together the warring academic forces.

Yet there is still a long way to go to establish an effective relation between the recruitment, prior preparation, induction, supervision, promotion, and continued education of teachers. The first steps of collaboration between the several parts of the college and university world to do a better job of preparation are under way, encouraged by private foundations and government. Teacher institutions are increasingly available to keep the teacher up to date in his subject and techniques. New organizational arrangements are sprouting up across the country. But these forces have not combined into a common approach, with one reinforcing the other to assure a higher quality of teaching performance.

The final test to be put on the quality of teaching—and therefore on the programs affecting teachers—is necessarily what the student learns.

The teacher and the classroom are, after all, means to an end, and not the end itself. The end of education is learning; if teaching does not achieve that consequence it is futile. Each new program for reform must finally stand or fall on its proven quality of attainment. Too often a plan for improving the effectiveness of teaching is judged on the basis of its intrinsic appeal, its inner logic; too rarely is it judged in terms of the actual learning of children, the intended product of the educational enterprise. In the necessary revolution of education, the means must become consistent with the end.

VII Quality in Education: The Curriculum

More than one observer has commented that the only generalization possible about American education is that no generalization is possible. There seems to be no national policy, no central administrative control, no single method of finance, no common practice in the classroom. The graduates differ widely in academic and social ability. To the extent that this first and negative generalization is correct, the search for an American *paideia* on the model of Jaeger's definition may seem a vain effort. And yet the same observer will comment— perhaps unfavorably—on the similarity of American life induced by a common culture and common communications.

Such considerations inevitably raise the question of what should be taught, and there are many questions about the curriculum that absorb the attention of educators today. Parents have heard about some of them, such as the new mathematics, and even worse have been asked to help with their child's homework. The curriculum in the schools is in flux. Which subjects should take priority? How should science be taught? Should languages be begun in the primary grades? Which of the many competitive methods for teaching reading are the most effective? These are only a sample of the questions that reflect profound change in the content and methods of learning.

This book does not try to deal with the curriculum by assessing the merits of such controversies. It is concerned rather with the question of how to assess the over-all quality of education available to America's children, and with the experiments and research that promise to raise that quality. It is concerned further with the question of whether the provision of equality of opportunity to all children will endanger the level of quality, and it argues that the national interest requires that American education seek and maintain equality and quality simultaneously.

Before the turn of the twentieth century, only a small group of reformers and psychologists in the United States ventured to question the dogma that the classical curriculum was the best road for the improvement of all minds. Even scientific thinking was only in its infancy. Later, the combined impact of the collegiate "free elective" system, the social need for training in vocational skills, and the measurement of differing "mental abilities" on the thinking of the teacher was almost incalculable. There seemed no longer to be a royal road to the progress of the individual or the society. In order to retain the idea of perfectibility and progress, these forces seemed to say, a new doctrine adjusted to individual talents and weaknesses had to be created. In the house of education there would have to be many mansions.

This notion of individual adjustment was not easy on the teacher or the society. A task that was formerly clear had become confused. Nor was it easy really to believe that all the educational roads to betterment were of equal value to the society, or deserved equal prestige. Brought up themselves in the tradition which put high social value on literary and mathematical (and later scientific) subjects, the majority of teachers in the depths of their feelings could not feel that teaching vocational subjects or tutoring the educationally disadvantaged was of equal value to the more familiar school subjects. While granting that some children needed help and special courses, the majority of teachers in mid-century were nevertheless only partly persuaded that the schools should take responsibility for the fact that the accident of inherited ability or social standing should govern (as they undoubtedly did in part) the pupil's future chances of success in society. Many doubted that it was the task of the schools to use the curriculum as an instrument of social reform. So did a substantial part of the public served by the schools.

The fundamental nature of the disagreements that grew from such uncertainties and doubts lay far beyond the curriculum itself. They grew from the shift of focus from the idea that this life is but the preparation for the next, to a focus on education as the best means of achieving a kind of progress here on earth. The idea of perfectibility was born under the former star, in earlier years. Could it now be hitched into the terrestial orbit? Were there only limited kinds of perfectibility possible to many humans on earth, and must we adjust our educational system to this undeniable, if unwelcome, fact?

Many of those who answer yes have said that there is no use pretending that some of the curricula that result are "as good" as others, and that separate schools had to be set up for separate purposes. In the large cities such arrangements were made, in such areas as science, or vocational education, or for the socially maladjusted. But the majority trend of thinking both by the public and the educators seemed to favor a variety of programs within the same high school, with a good deal of common experience for all students. This became the comprehensive high school, the twentieth-century version of the old idea of the common school. Here the pupils could, if they wished and if they improved their ability to learn, move from one kind of program to another. Such a pattern of flexibility took care of two objections which were made to the idea of curricula linked directly to individual differences: the objection that no test of native ability was really accurate since many tests fail to allow for cultural differences, and therefore that fixed assignments to particular curricula might penalize children who might improve as they grew older. The system of flexibility gave room for the powers of moral courage to come to play. It allowed the effects of sheer hard work and persistence to be felt. In short, it made it more nearly possible for citizen and educator alike to say that each child while in school had equal opportunity—which is to say that the school was carrying out its part of the bargain with the idea of perfectibility and the idea of education for all. And the onus of decision was left, at least in theory, to the individual, not to society operating through the teacher.

At this point it is worth pointing out that this policy of flexibility marked off the American system of education from the system operating in other parts of the world through most of the century. Outside of the United States it was normal to decide at eleven or twelve years whether a child should undertake the rigors of the academic program which led to the professions. If not, he was directed into separate programs in general or vocational schools leading to the several trades and occupations. (Exceptions were made, of course, where the parents of the child could afford private education.) The chances of changing from one program to the other were apparently small, after that time. Once a selected group had been formed, it became possible to require a common curriculum and rate of work since the students were more nearly homogeneous in both their aspirations and their abilities. Rapid progress along the desired path was possible. Laggards were not admitted to slow down the majority.

In the United States, on the other hand, the decision on the type of school program to be undertaken was delayed a few years, with most students making a selection after the age of fourteen. The nation has only recently come to see that children of the disadvantaged have the decision thrust upon them much earlier, perhaps even before they enter school at all. Yet for the majority, there was an atmosphere within most schools and colleges which encouraged students to change from one area to another. A guidance counselor who finds a pupil with a high IQ who is not in the academic curriculum will encourage him to make the shift. The fact that there are a good many opportunities for children in different programs to be taught together has tended to reduce, though by no means eliminate, the social differences among the several groups within the school.

All these factors combined to make it difficult to create a classroom of pupils with common aspirations and abilities and, above all, with common achievement. One result was that the students in the academic curricula in the United States were less advanced than their selected counterparts in Europe. They may have learned more in some areas, they may have been better adjusted socially (evidence on these topics is notoriously hard to compare), but they were seriously believed to be behind in such areas as the use of foreign languages, the grasp of history, and the like.

The compromise, the *modus vivendi,* however, made it possible for the teacher to carry on with both the assumption of education for all, and the optimistic assumption about the nature of man. Underneath the disputes about the details of the curriculum, a common set of assumptions, rarely mentioned in practice, bound the schools together. This common climate of thought accounted for the observation that despite admistrative variation, despite lack of unified direction, there was a common quality to American schooling. Remove the assumptions and the American school system would change its tone. This is but another way of saying that the schools were and are deeply embedded in the American religious and political tradition. The common beliefs underlying one aspect of that tradition, the belief in the goodness of man and in the possibility of progress, are the support of the schools, and increasingly of the colleges as well. Flexibility of program and an acceptance of new subjects, though with an uneasy mind, have been the hallmarks of the American attitude toward the curriculum.

By mid-century the question of equality of the chance for learning was raised even more insistently. The scientific competition with other nations caused many to wonder if the schools were finding the talented and demanding enough of them. The needs of a rapidly changing economy required ever higher standards of performance on jobs that called for academic skills. The vision of the Great Society, and the tragic condition of the poor and the minority groups which that vision brought into focus for all to see, insisted on a reassessment of what the schools were teaching. The *modus vivendi* was being sharply questioned. What were the facts? How well did children learn? Was there a real equality of opportunity for a high quality of education or was it being hidden by a compromise of curricula?

It became clear that American education had not yet faced up to the question of how to determine the quality of academic performance in the schools. There was a lack of information. Without a reporting system that alerted state or federal authorities to the need for support to shore up educational weakness, programs had to be devised on the basis of social and economic data. In these areas, on the other hand, the nation was fairly well informed about the state of affairs. The Bureau of Labor Statistics made available employment figures, and the government, therefore, had a sound foundation for response to news of rising unemployment in particular industries and in particular communities. Economic reports existed on family needs, but no data existed to supply similar facts on the quality and condition of what children learned. The nation could find out about school buildings or discover how many years children stay in school; it had no satisfactory way of assessing whether the time spent in school was effective.

Yet if it was in the national interest for the federal government to ease unemployment, to control recessions and inflation, it was also in the national interest to know whether its children were learning well enough to adjust to the changing economy. In both areas the public sector was related to the private sector; in the field of economics, the public sector expressed its concern through interest-rate control, budgeting, and reducing or increasing its own expenditures. It could only do so on the basis of detailed knowledge, not guesswork. The public sector had the same requirement for a reporting system in education. The need was seen, and was reflected in the requirements for reports in the education legislation of the mid-1960's. But the method of collecting data became a subject of debate. The Carnegie Corporation of New York, a private philanthropic foundation, with government encouragement undertook to explore methods of testing selected samples of children, under contracts with private organizations, in order to work out ways of determining, for example, how rapidly children had learned to read, whether they had learned to write coherent paragraphs, whether they understood fundamental principles of science, whether they were grasping the concepts embodied in the Constitution. The methods chosen were designed to avoid the dangers involved in testing all pupils—the dangers of imposing a rigid curriculum and encouraging teachers to teach pupils to prepare for a test rather than to learn a subject.

The very question of measuring the results of schooling has to be considered against the American method of deciding what should be taught in schools, and what standards should be established, and by whom. For neither federal nor (in most cases) state agencies are involved with matters of curricula or testing. No single agency or group sets minimum standards of pupil accomplishment. No national or regional testing results are widely used. No group of colleges or universities maintains an admission standard for preparation in certain subjects which in effect controls the academic curriculum as is in general true in Europe and England.

Only the State of New York requires that some pupils be tested against a state standard established in the Regents' examination, and many local school systems could scarcely be said to like that arrangement. The College Entrance Examination Board, which is used by a substantial number of colleges and universities for admission purposes, does not view its task as in any sense setting standards but rather as a source of information to schools and colleges about individual achievement. Colleges and universities vary so widely in aim and practice that no common requirements are enforced.

As a result the standards required in elementary and secondary schools vary enormously, and are controlled by the attitudes of large numbers of teachers and administrators, influenced by a variety of forces rather than by any central source. Among these forces are the departments and schools of education of the colleges and universities and the dwindling number of teachers' colleges.

These departments and schools of education do more than train personnel in schools. They also help to create a climate of thought. Since the early part of the twentieth century, they have strayed far from the paths usually associated with the normal schools, no longer content, as in the nineteenth-century pattern, to teach subject matter primarily. They have become increasingly concerned with problems of the schools in the social order. They concern themselves with the curriculum, which once rested largely in the hands of the college groups. They consider the interaction of economic and social forces and the school as an institution. They engage in research in psychology and related fields. They contemplate the nature of man and of the society and propose ways in which education and the schools can play a part in improving that society. They seek to learn more about the children whom society has neglected, the more fully to understand the gap between this "deviant" culture and American middle class life. They are, in short—or can be—the very centers of that belief in the idea of the man's natural capacity for good, and that faith in progress, which has earlier been described as the foundation stone of the public school system.

The colleges and universities, apart from their departments or schools of education, in the past concentrated on only one aspect of the school's curriculum: that which avowedly prepared the students for college admission. Prior to 1900, the wishes of college teachers had a governing influence over the high school curriculum. Since a substantial group of high school students of that day planned to carry on their education at the college level, such an arrangement was only natural. College faculties conducted a holding operation until the late 1950's, feeling that they were losing ground year by year, for as the high schools expanded, a smaller percentage of their graduates was capable of or interested in a classical education. The curriculum became subject to other, more local influences. Teachers in the schools came to have fewer official and personal connections with their colleagues in the colleges. College admission requirements were fought by the high schools and sometimes ignored. Emphasis on vocational education helped to build between the two groups of educators a barrier of social class which many teachers found it hard to scale. In time the colleges came to have influence only in the college preparatory aspect of the curriculum, and even this influence tended to weaken as the years went by.

Such developments did not take place without comment. The history of the National Education Association records a bitter struggle between the school and the college groups, which is still reflected in national organizations of educators. The tendency in the academic world to identify this struggle as one between the advocate of the "liberal arts" and the proponent of the "professional" education point of view obscures a more important issue, for collegiate and university groups are in touch with a wide variety of regional and national interests. Compared with the educator who deals only with the problems of the local primary and the secondary schools, college personnel are in a better position to apply influence at the several levels of government and of private enterprise, both through their regular programs and through the influence of their alumni. By allowing a sharp separation between college and school personnel (and it should here be noted that the teachers' colleges and the schools of education are identified as being on the side of the schools and not the colleges) the entire group of educators permitted division in their own ranks to weaken their total influence. This division goes a long way toward explaining why the educators, despite their great numbers and their geographical coverage, have had less voice in public affairs than any group of comparable size with special interests in contemporary society.

By and large the defensive posture of the college faculties kept them from taking an active part in influencing the curriculum for the great majority of students who do not plan to go to college. The interests of school teachers and administrators, and through them of the professors of education, were well represented at the state and local level, but the interests of the specialists in the various fields of human knowledge were not. Since there was little formal machinery for the latter to exercise this influence through established channels—state, national, or professional groups—it can be said that the United States presented the ironic situation of a nation dependent on its scholars and specialists but denying them much voice in planning how the subject they knew best would be interpreted to the coming generation. Nor did they have much opportunity to consider how their specialty should be interrelated to the general body of knowledge and skills taught by the public schools. The engineer, for example, had relatively little to say about the nature of the ordinary program of vocational teaching in the high school. The lawyer had little chance to affect the textbook on civics. The professor of literature no longer chose the prose and poetry used in the general courses in English. So matters stood in the late 1950's.

This remarkable pattern of diffusion of control and voluntarism in association and in standards was and is the essential framework of American education. Complex administration and variability of procedure are the inevitable result.

For the American vision of what the nation's schools should accomplish is as big as the sky itself. The vision is the result of no planned design. It is an accumulation of aims, each forged from some social need, each with its army of devoted supporters. The aims of American education have been formed by a process of accretion, not selection, and the curriculum of the high school became closer to a smorgasbord than to an Escoffier dinner. The American people, blessed with incomparable wealth and characteristic optimism, have in effect allowed each man to have his choice. They have piled upon the schools a thousand tasks. By their pattern of local control they have assured that no national policy and pattern can be set by central authority. And by the very lack of that central design they have assured that the inherent conflicts of assumptions under which their schools are told to operate could be buried in the confusion of practice. The vast instrument operates in a common direction only because of the dedication of its participants to certain common ideals and beliefs and the existence of certain common bonds.

Yet from this situation one fact emerges. If schools are to find their proper place in the society, and if they are to respond to social changes, more will be needed than an understanding only of *how* children learn certain subjects. The nation will have to know how *well* they learn. The school is the product of many social and intellectual forces, each with a long tradition and each with a different impact on the daily work of the teacher and student in the classroom. Philosophy and history, sociology and political science, anthropology and psychology, are all grist to the mill of educational policy. The study of education in a democracy is the study of preparing man for a new setting, and the application of what is learned has to be related to the facts about the setting. It seems clear that some solution has to be found to the problem of inadequate data on educational results, whether or not the Carnegie program wins support, and however lively the debate on methods becomes.

Changing social and economic facts of the mid-century caused debate in American education not only about standards of student performance but also about the breadth and depth of the curriculum. Has the American secondary school curriculum been in the past too unimaginative, too limited? Many pioneers in curriculum reform were scholars in the several disciplines, who seldom before had concerned themselves with primary or secondary school education. Their experimentation suggested that children would learn more rapidly and follow more complex reasoning than educators had previously supposed. Their conclusions suggested, in turn, a revised and more daring curriculum.

Some bold experiments were under way in curriculum reform. The decade of the late 1950's and early 1960's saw a lively reappraisal of the educational system in an effort to extend the frontiers of learning. The preliminary results suggested unexpected possibilities for the future, and deserve reporting.

In some schools two- and three-year olds were being taught to read and write; first-graders were being asked to deal with the fundamentals of economics and algebra; second- and third-graders were exploring concepts of relativity physics and learning to write music; fourth- and fifth-graders were encouraged to "discover" set theory in mathematics; junior high school students explored anthropological concepts; and high school students studied physics and literature in courses formerly taught only in college.

These were dramatic developments in themselves, for they suggested the possibilities of educational improvement in a new age of learning, constantly seeking the unknown limits of the human mind.

The Office of Education supported projects to prepare new content for the teaching of the arts, the languages and composition, the social studies, and the vocational and technical subjects. The National Science Foundation made grants to support new school curricula in mathematics, the biological sciences, and the physical sciences. Experimentation and the testing of new materials not only received active federal support but received it on a far larger scale than ever before. And so did the training of teachers in these subjects. Scholars and educators joined forces—though not always amicably— to bring the schools new ways of approaching old subjects. No one could tell how well the new programs would look later, for a long period of trial by the fire of the classroom lay ahead. The particular fashion of today might be, as it has been so often before, forgotten tomorrow. But innovation and change themselves became fashionable and, with the encouragement of federal dollars and the interest of the scholarly and scientific community as well as the leaders in the schools, the dawn of a new era could be seen.

Names little known to school teachers and administrators in 1955 were widely discussed ten years later. In Cambridge, Massachusetts, a group of physicists under the direction of Jerrold Zacharias had developed a new physics course designed to revise and update high school study of physical science for those planning to go on to technical and scientific careers. This was a significant departure in curriculum development, for it involved university scientists of great distinction directly in the process of preparing materials and techniques for the schools.

A major program was undertaken by the School Mathematics Study Group, and the letters SMSG could be heard in discussions at teachers' meetings. The Office of Education undertook to support Project English and Project Social Studies—the very use of the word "project" was significant—and the private philanthropic foundations became active participants in the reform movement.

At Yale, at Rutgers, and more recently in the Educational Research and Development Center at Pittsburgh, social psychologist O. K. Moore has demonstrated in an experimental program that children as young as two can be taught to read by using their own natural curiosity and drive. At Purdue, economist Lawrence Senesh has taught fundamentals of college-level economics to second-graders and brought them to solving real economic problems.

At the Julliard School of Music in New York City, composer-conductor Vittorio Giannini has worked with a team of musicians, composers, and music teachers to enrich the repertory of elementary school music courses. At Stanford University, philosopher-mathematician Patrick Suppes has taught advanced algebra to fifth-graders, and Nobel Prize winner William Shockley has introduced the concept of conservation of energy to ninth-graders.

At the University of California in Berkeley, Sinclair Lewis' biographer, Mark Schorer, has worked on new techniques for teaching poetry, drama, the short story, and the novel in the early grades.

Such a listing of projects could not have been made in the early 1950's, nor such a listing of scientists and scholars engaged in curriculum reform. A new era seems to have dawned for the schools. For if children can learn in grade school what was formerly introduced to them in college, it would appear that the schools have been underestimating for generations the learning capacity of children. They may have wasted time and talent, and therefore wasted important resources of any society.

Many of these experiments seemed also to lead to more than a deepening and enriching the content of the curriculum; they suggested re-evaluation of the definition of education. There developed an attitude that education was not only a memorizing of facts and rules, easily forgotten, but rather a training of the mind to weigh facts, to arrive at rules by testing hypotheses—a training of the mind to understand. These were scarcely new insights, of course. But the fact that it could be practical to carry out such a definition of education into practice with large numbers of students has excited the educational world, encouraging a new look at the schools.

Every age has given its own answers to the curricular question, and in every age notable men have quarreled over those answers. Socrates felt that philosophy was an unsuitable study for young men because they were too hot-blooded to bring to the study of ideas the spirit of cool deliberation that philosophy demands. Sir Philip Sidney defended the study of poetry on the grounds that poetry made it easier for young people to remember moral sentiments; Benjamin Franklin saw value in the mechanical arts despite the grave doubts of his contemporaries.

To the contemporary debate was added the voice of the psychologist. Knowledge, he said, takes on greater meaning if it has been gained through struggle and self-questioning, rather than through passive acceptance. If the learner has the right to accept or reject ideas in terms of the understanding they contribute to him, then the knowledge that he does acquire is more functionally available than if he had it simply passed on to him. Learning in schools, many psychologists and reformers argued, was often more a conforming than a creative process.

To establish the spirit of inquiry in the curriculum, they posed three assumptions:

1. Students must have an intellectual challenge by bringing them into direct and repeated confrontation with the gaps and inadequacies in their knowledge and understanding, both to incite their curiosity and to invite them to search for ideas and principles that explain the data they are trying to relate.
2. Students need access to raw data and to the ideas of others by bringing the learner close to the world outside. This implies more exposure to uninterpreted things, places, people, and documents.
3. Inquiry demands independence. Schools have to offer the learner freedom to gather and process data. This implies setting aside timetables of content coverage.

Each of these conditions dealt less with the question of which subjects ought to be covered and more with the question of *approach* to content. Concern with the curriculum became related, as it had so often before in history, with psychological theory and school practice. And it was not long before the broader issues of social philosophy and the goals of the society came into focus. What was, after all, the purpose of teaching certain subjects? To bring out of the individual his special talents, and to build upon them to his personal fulfillment? Or to meet the needs of a society that demanded well-trained manpower for jobs whose nature and number were hard to predict? Or to prepare citizens for their duties as voters in a world that demanded ever more wisdom and special knowledge?

The answer, of course, to all these questions was yes. A choice could not be made. And the reformers had to work out their answers in the light of the realities of mid-century society, not as an abstract exercise. They had to take into account the unhappy fact that certain curricula in practice seemed to be used primarily for pupils from certain social classes or even racial groups. Equality of educational opportunity did not square with type of program or quality of offering. New curricula would have to be brought in line with social goals and educational realities as well as with advances in knowledge and new psychological theories of learning. It was not only that new approaches in particular subjects—mathematics or history or physics—were needed; such approaches had to be related in new ways to one another and to the values of the society in which the learners lived. Simply to reform a particular course might not have a lasting effect. What was needed was the larger view of the curriculum as a whole, of the forest rather than only the trees.

For this purpose the entire capacity of the educational, scholarly, and productive sectors of society had to be tapped, and means worked out to assure collaboration. Past history offered few guides. Quarrels between professional educators and scholars had to be patched up, and the interest of entire university faculties brought to bear on curricular problems. A new relationship with the industry that produced teaching materials was required.

Merely to add new subjects and materials on top of the old was no longer possible. A method of making choices had to be worked out, involving all the forces that influence curriculum change: the needs of the individual learner, the needs of the society for an educated citizenry, the demands of a changing economy, the effects of the advance of knowledge, the social goals of a democracy. The new partnership of federal, state, local, and private interests clearly had its work cut out for it in facing the coming revolution. The requirements of the larger view thrust the role of the national interest into center stage. Whether or not local school boards liked it, decisions on what should be taught could no longer be their exclusive affair. If curricular policy was too important to be left only to the educators, as many had long agreed, it had now become too important to be left only in local hands.

VIII Quality in Education: Research, Development, and the Instruments of Learning

Two antithetical factors—a distaste for innovation on the one hand, and an exaggerated craving for fashionable ideas, on the other—have disrupted and hobbled the effectiveness of modern educational research and reform. By the 1960's, however, the nation seemed to have made a new start on an old problem. In most of the educational acts of the Congress there were provisions for research, either as a major thrust of the program or as an integral part of its operation. Even more important was the realization that education would have to change the scale of its thinking on how to bring about the revolution in its practices that the future demanded. Small projects with no provision for testing or demonstration were no longer enough—if they ever were. Education was entering an age in which scattered efforts at change must be joined. The innovations of recent years, many of them supported by the private foundations, showed that change was possible. But as one looks at the record of each, it is clear that each was trying by itself, often without adequate funding, to bring about a change which could only be done together.

The next step had to be the working out not only of particular innovations but of *systems* of change. Equipment must be linked to curricula, teaching methods to school organization, and all four to the preparation of teachers and to measures of the results in what pupils learn. The scattered bits had to be drawn together. This was a task for which the educational research community was not prepared by habit or experience, as were the research communities in military affairs, in agriculture, in space exploration, or in manifold aspects of modern industry. New research laboratories funded by the government were designed to help start the process of preparing for the future. But it would not be wise to rely on the government alone in an area so essential to the oncoming revolution in quality of education. The private sector of the economy, which provides the materials for learning, has a role to play beyond merely filling orders. As in other aspects of the society's life, it too could invest funds in research and development.

There is good reason for industry, commerce, and labor to be concerned with bringing about the revolution in educational practice. Although no one has estimated accurately the annual cost of training programs for personnel carried on outside schools and colleges, it surely runs well into the billions of dollars a year. The private sector has its own concern with raising the quality of the education of its work force. It needs new materials or combinations of materials for its own sake, as well as for the sake of doing business with the schools.

Just as important is the contribution the private sector can make through its know-how in the organization and management of research and development enterprises and in distributing their results. In an area where education has little experience, the private sector is knowledgeable and well staffed. It can contribute to the strengthening of both public affairs and private profit by taking an active part in the development of new ways of teaching and learning, and above all in working out new, interrelated systems using different types of educational equipment and methods in combination. And there are those who feel that the private sector can also serve as a countervailing force both to stimulate and to act as a balance against governmental activities. In addition, then, to the new partnership being forged among the several levels of government to carry out educational change, the necessary revolution must also call upon a new partnership between the public and the private sectors of the economy in educational research and development.

For Americans live in an era when research and development are greatly esteemed in industry, in technology, in medicine—in almost every major enterprise but education, where research has long been undervalued and underfinanced. A few American industries spend up to 10 percent of their gross revenues on research and development. In 1965, the federal government alone spent almost a billion dollars on medical research and nearly $200 million on agricultural research.

But where did the nation stand in regard to public schools, an enterprise which stood at the base of research for knowledge and the development of human talent?

Education was in a sense America's largest industry in the mid-1960's—with 123,000 schools, 55 million school pupils and college students, almost 2.4 million teachers, 100,000 administrators and supervisors, and 144 thousand local public school board members. In an enterprise costing $39 billion a year at all levels, the nation spent less than one-half of 1 percent of its educational funds on research to improve the educational process itself.

This figure—one-half of 1 percent—was not a figure from the distant past but an improvement on the recent past. It represents the funds the nation spent on research at a time when it at last was beginning to get educational research under way. It included the new research funds voted by the Education Congress in 1965. But it did not include the promise of new private investment.

The ingredients of the new mix began in the middle 1960's. Large private corporations have begun to purchase publishing firms, and several have announced plans to explore the possibility of linking the conventional text materials to the newer ideas of teaching machines, audio-visual aids, and automatic data processing. For the first time large supplies of capital from the private sector of the economy have become potentially available for research and development into new ways of providing instruments of learning. One observer of the scene, Dean Theodore Sizer of Harvard, regards the development as comparable in importance to the expanding role of the federal government in education. He foresaw both promise and risk in his annual report for 1964–65:

Earlier I mentioned that the shift in control of educational policy was not limited to the gravitation towards Washington, but included changes in the private sector as well. The recognition both of the increased interest in and money for support of education by all levels of government and of the growth of the school population has prompted businesses not previously in the "education industry" to consider entering this high potentional market. Further, the development of new technical devices—teaching machines, audio and visual equipment of great sophistication, computer-based teaching systems, and the rest—has attracted companies previously uninterested in the schools. The level of interest is well exemplified by the plans of the American Management Association for a large conference on the issue in early July of 1965.

Schools have traditionally been supplied by relatively small and specialized companies. The textbook industry is by and large distinct. There are concerns which produce films, others for equipment. Most of these companies have never put much emphasis on research. Few have attempted coordination or merger with other segments of the school supply industry.

The entrance of new kinds of companies will change this situation dramatically, for the newcomers are large companies, with traditions of research and of broad scale operation. The list now includes Xerox, Time, Raytheon, and International Business Machines and will surely grow. These parent companies are buying smaller firms in the various aspects of the education industry and will present in due time a coordinated line of teaching materials and equipment to the schools.

The potential virtue of this coordination is great. Books and films and teaching machines and the rest can be related as never before and can provide for teachers a lift comparable to the introduction of free textbooks in the 1890's. The potential dangers are no less obvious. As with federal dollars coming before ideas for their use, in the education industry we have technical devices of great sophistication before we have clear ends, much less materials, for them. We have better teaching machines than programs for them, better educational television equipment than ideas on how to use it. The new companies are as impatient as the administrators in Washington, and we run the risk of having the schools inundated with quantities of technically exciting but intellectually inadequate materials.

If Dean Sizer was right, and there were many who agreed with him, a radical change was likely to take place in the instruments of learning available to the schools of the second half of the century as a result of new programs and new materials. Their influence could be incalculable. And their content became a major problem. The sense of responsibility to high quality rather than shoddy goods had to be shared between the public and the private sectors. To accomplish this goal required more than self-regulation by a new industry, though that clearly was a consideration. It required also a new sense of responsibility by the academic community, for which Dean Sizer pleaded elsewhere in his report. And the government had to enter the field because of its decision to finance research and development in education on a scale only dreamed of by a few in the 1950's. The budget for research in the Office of Education in the fiscal year 1966 was nearly $100 million, one hundred times larger than a decade before, and four times larger than the prior year. The office's decision to place the results of its research activities into the public domain set up one guideline to its future relation to the private sector: the government wanted to encourage competition in the use of new ideas and programs.

Chart 9. Office of Education financial assistance for educational research

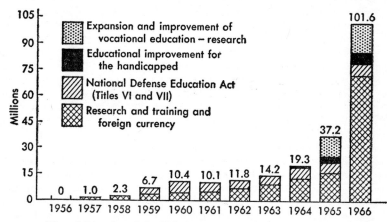

SOURCE: Office of Education of the U.S. Department of Health, Education, and Welfare.

For the act of financing research, in itself, is no panacea for the educational problems of the future. Equally important in a decentralized system is to stimulate a willingness to test the results of research, to put into practice the best of tested innovations. To this end, research and demonstration centers were established in 1964 at several universities across the country. New regional laboratories were on the drawing boards in 1965, designed to serve education much as the agricultural experiment centers long served and stimulated the development of agriculture.

Four modest and necessarily incomplete forerunners of the proposed Regional Educational Laboratories were operating by 1965 financed by the Office of Education. They performed only some of the functions to be handled by the laboratories, but they nonetheless served as pilot efforts for a new and continuous effort. A center in Pittsburgh, for example, put research on basic learning into practice in the schools. Recognizing that the ability of children of the same age in the same classroom often differs by as much as four or five grade levels, Pittsburgh provided programs of individualized instruction based on capacity rather than age.

A center at the University of Oregon studied the structure of school-community relations and the way educational policies are formed and decisions are put into effect. The center explored the relationship between school improvement, sources of financial assistance, and community involvement in educational planning.

At the center at the University of Wisconsin, researchers, scholars, and teachers worked as a team on the central problems of learning—how, how much, how early, how quickly, and how well children can learn. They were developing programs of education, based upon this research, designed to introduce subjects and materials at the most opportune time in the child's development.

A center at Harvard University concerned itself with problems presented by psychological and cultural differences among school children. It secured the cooperation of the school systems in Boston, Cambridge, Newton, Concord, and Lexington. Two local school superintendents were members of the seven-member executive committee of the Harvard Research and Development Center. This cooperation explored the working relationships which might emerge from the partnership of Regional Educational Laboratories and supplementary education centers and services, as provided under Titles III and IV of the Elementary and Secondary Education Act.

The Research and Development Centers were not the only institutions which suggest possible models for aspects of the future in educational research. Emerging forms of interuniversity cooperation and school and university partnerships that already existed also contained functions and patterns of operation which could fit into a major laboratory enterprise.

The first year of operation of the Office of Education Research and Development Centers confirmed a hope that large-scale program centers of educational research were feasible and could lead to improved educational programs. It also showed the possibility of mobilizing all levels of education to improve educational technology and to do so more effectively and with greater economy of resources. But four centers alone, with all their promise, could not serve the needs of 27,000 school districts, the needs of 2,600 institutions of higher learning, or the fifty states and many regions of the country. A network that linked every stage from basic research to product, from the original idea to education practice, had to be forged.

The task which faces American education is of such proportions that there will have to be at least ten to fifteen major laboratories— and perhaps more in time—devoted to full-time innovation, experimentation, and dissemination. In 1965, the Congress appropriated $45 million for this purpose, so it could be said that the process was under way. But far more has to be worked out, for these future laboratories may vary not only in location but in form and function, size and staff.

Yet they will clearly have certain common characteristics. Essential are close ties with the educational system at all levels, coordination with state departments of education, and the availability of research personnel from the academic world and industry.

Each laboratory will have to be associated with one or more schools or local school systems where laboratory-tested techniques and programs can be tried out and evaluated on a large scale. Cooperation and continuous communication among laboratories will be required. For example, an experimental school serving one laboratory might well serve in a similar capacity to several or all other laboratories on a particular topic. This association with schools and school systems can provide the link that has been missing for years between proposal and practice, a missing link that is in good part responsible for education's reputation for resistance to innovation.

Staff for the laboratories will have to be drawn from a variety of sources. The interdisciplinary attack on educational problems was a relatively new and successful strategy in educational reform by the mid-1960's. The National Science Foundation and the Office of Education had supported projects in which competent scholars in several

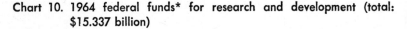

Chart 10. 1964 federal funds* for research and development (total: $15.337 billion)

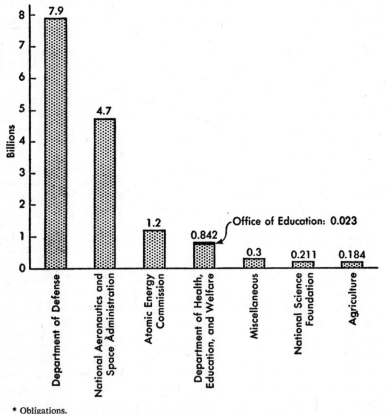

* Obligations.
SOURCE: "Federal Funds for Research, Development, and Other Scientific Activities, 1964," National Science Foundation.

fields worked side by side with local school personnel and educators. Together they produced new instructional materials, laboratory equipment, textbooks, teacher guides, and films, tried them out, and tested them in selected schoolrooms. Early results showed increases in the depth and quality of learning. The new laboratories could be expected to continue these efforts, but on a far larger scale. Artists, historians, mathematicians, and other scholars could be allied with psychologists, sociologists, teachers, and administrators from local school systems to develop and evaluate curricula and other educational programs.

To provide research personnel needed in the years ahead, training opportunities will have to be created at the laboratories and at other institutions throughout the nation. As new research programs appear and as present ones grow, the need for qualified personnel will become critical.

The centers already established at universities, and the laboratories of the future have a variety of materials to work with; they are not without new ideas or new techniques to develop, test, and refine.

Teaching machines are an example. The term became familiar to the reader of newspapers or family magazines in the early 1960's. The publicity given them too often created the impression that they could solve all problems of educational quality; for that very reason, many dismissed them as just another kind of gadget. Yet a teaching machine was simply a piece of equipment: it had no more inherent force than a blackboard or a piece of chalk. What mattered was the written program that went *into* the machine and the use to which it was put. The more accurate title was therefore "programmed instruction," a way to bring the student into the development of an idea step by step, and give him a way to check his own progress. The purpose was to make him realize his successes and his errors as soon as he made them—not days later when the quizzes were returned. The best programs mimicked the methods of a good teacher, but had the advantage of allowing each student to progress at his own speed. In theory, therefore, the quick pupils were not bored by being held back to a common pace, and the slow not embarrassed or discouraged by their slower rate of learning. These machines, whether in the form of boxes or books, seemed particularly adaptable to the study of subjects easily broken down into elemental steps—grammar, foreign language study, elementary logic, or mathematics. Doubts were expressed as to whether they were useful in subjects where "right" answers are not as available, as in ethics, metaphysics, history (beyond the acquisition of facts), appreciation of poetry and art, and critical understanding of complex ideas.

Yet there was much to learn about how to program such instruction and how to use mechanical equipment effectively with the students. Basic questions needed answers as well. Was the psychological theory sound? Would the step-by-step progression to "right" answers prove as rigid, as dogmatic, and stultifying as the recitation of facts by a teacher? Would it fail to stimulate the spirit of inquiry itself by discarding the possibility of alternatives, by discouraging the experience of error, by encouraging the assumption that all knowledge is gained by simple steps? Would it in fact free the teacher to give more attention to individual students, or make him expendable? There were many questions to ask, much research to be done—yet the concept clearly showed promise. An instrument seemed at hand to strengthen the teacher's arm, if he was not frightened of its risks.

In the case of audio-visual devices, another relatively new instrument of learning, experience had proved them useful in a number of areas of the curriculum. The focus in foreign languages, for example, shifted in the fifties away from the primary goal of enabling the student to read a foreign language, to the more comprehensive goal of teaching him to understand, write, and speak it as well. The range of languages themselves broadened. Russian and Chinese were added to the usual Spanish and French in some schools.

Tape recorders were used successfully to permit the student to hear a foreign language as it is spoken by natives, not as processed by a teacher who might contribute his or her own regional twang to the umlaut or *accent grave*. In electronic classrooms and language laboratories, the teacher listened as students practiced pronunciation individually, and evaluated their progress and corrected mistakes along the way, as in the meantime other students continued their own practice.

Foreign-language laboratory installations in public high schools increased from forty-six in 1958 to more than 7,000 in 1965. This increase came about principally as a result of funds provided by the federal government under the National Defense Education Act of 1958. Yet such installations would have to be increased at least fivefold to give listening-speaking practice daily to half of the high school population.

Other uses of audio-visual materials in other subjects and of other types were made, and more could be expected. Yet exciting though many of these new teaching devices became, they were available generally only to schools in comfortable communities. The nation's rural and ghetto schools—where good and imaginative equipment was most needed—were the most deprived. It became the task of the new federal, state, and local partnership to redress the balance as well as to explore the wider use of the media.

Educational television presented another instrument capable of exposing students to new ideas. Little more than ten years after the government decided to reserve a percentage of the television spectrum for noncommercial educational use there were more than a hundred of these reserved channels operating throughout the country. About three-fourths of the stations broadcast programs directly into school and college classrooms throughout the school day. Estimates indicated that upwards of ten million students received a part of their formal education through television. In half a dozen large cities where daily instructional programs place a heavy tax on available station time, a second station has been licensed to take care of the heavy traffic load.

Activity, of course, is not the same as significance. Educational television soon showed that it was no substitute for a teacher; its value seemed to be in enabling a fine teacher to teach many more students at a time than could be gathered in one classroom, and to widen the range of what could be brought to the student's attention. Films, of course, had the same advantages, but were said to lack the possibility of immediacy of impact and the chance for rapid feedback.

Research findings suggested that students learned as well, and in some instances better, from televised instruction as from conventional classroom teaching, under proper conditions of selection and use. As with virtually all the circumstances of the teaching situation, these conditions rested with the teacher and the mastery of the medium, whether the teacher was on camera or in the classroom.

Television by the early 1960's had earned its place as an important new instrument of learning. But its potential had not been fully tested, for its programs were uneven and its financing uncertain. The coming turn of the educational wheel might change its minor role to that of major participant.

However exciting new techniques might be for laboratories to study or educators to praise or denounce, the book remained the king. About 8 percent of the teaching staff of the public schools have to leave the classrooms every year. On the average the schools must then expect that every five years means a major change in personnel, with most of the new teachers both young and inexperienced. Under these circumstances it is easy to see—for this situation is not of recent origin—why there has long been a heavy reliance on text materials as the basis of the teachers' work. A single book, such as Webster's Primer or McGuffey's Reader, has guided generations of students— and of teachers. Its content has formed countless opinions. Indeed, Webster's text is considered by historians as an important factor in developing the idea of American nationalism.

The book, of course, is one of the oldest teaching machines known to man. The quality of American textbooks is often high, yet many have not kept pace with current knowledge or with the tempo of social change. Some tried to lead the way to new experimental curricula; many merely followed the safe road. Children used textbooks both out of date and inadequate for an era of expanding educational horizons. "Modern history" books often had nothing to teach our children about events after the First World War, and physics texts often dealt with the state of knowledge in the thirties and early forties—ignoring, for example, the atomic revolution.

The textbook and library provisions of the Elementary and Secondary Education Act of 1965 clearly were needed, both to provide funds for schools to purchase up-to-date materials and to encourage the publishing industry to embark on an era of new materials and new approaches. It was, of course, to the advantage of the publishers to supply in large quantity—to encourage school systems to use the same materials. The book salesman carried ideas and observations of practices wherever he went: like the *jongleur* of old, he brought tales of other lands. Since new practices mean new products and more business, he encouraged their wide dissemination, but only if they were in his line of goods. The books that he sold, often prepared in close collaboration with the schools, tended to set curricular patterns. And the books that he no longer found profitable by their very absence discouraged the teaching of their subject matter. Since teachers are human, the form and the approach used in the texts tended to guide actual practice in the classroom, and practice is reinforced by texts that are adapted to such practice. The informal atmosphere now so common in classrooms in the elementary schools, and the subdivision of pupils into constantly shifting small groups for common projects, would have been impossible without specially devised workbooks and without the movable type of desk. It was not

Chart 11. Office of Education financial assistance for public libraries

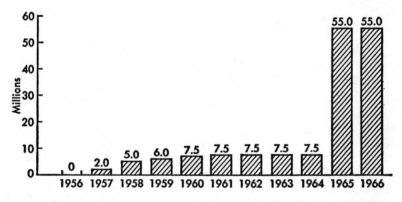

SOURCE: Office of Education of the U.S. Department of Health, Education and Welfare.

only the persuasiveness of the professors of elementary education which revolutionized these practices in the elementary schools in the past thirty years: the salesmen of texts played an essential role.

The influence of the textbook extended beyond particular content or educational technique in the classroom. A subcommittee of the Research Council of the Great Cities Program for School Improvement, for example, reported that "most textbook orientation appears to be toward the middle-class white, Anglo-Saxon Protestant." The psychological distance between the children of the poor and the school text was often great. The materials provided tended to make it hard to adjust teaching to the special needs of minority groups. New material was required.

And the year 1963 was cited as marking a revolution in the textbook industry, on the ground that it brought the first widespread publication of texts with "integrated illustration." A few of them, it was true, merely took the old texts and colored some of the white children brown, but others represented a far more basic response to the needs of minority groups. For the problem was not simply that of having minority groups appear on the page, but rather one of accurate interpretation of their problems in American society and of appropriate recognition of their role in American history.

Yet students do not learn, of course, from texts alone. Indeed the term "textbook" can be narrowly interpreted as meaning that special genre of books published especially for use in the classroom. For libraries also have long had a major role to play in the educational process. And Francis S. Chase of the University of Chicago stated the case for the future:

We have left the kind of world in which the teacher's chief function was to convey information. The school composed chiefly of classrooms is obsolete. In schools of the future, upwards of half of the student's time may be spent in the library, in science labratories, or in other workrooms where he can search for knowledge, analyze data, reflect upon the ideas which he is encountering, and put his hunches and conclusions in writing.

The school library will provide a variety of resources, including recordings, microfilms, slide films, videotapes, charts, maps and pictures. The most important of the resources offered, however, will be books in abundance in the humanities, the social studies, the sciences, and the practical arts—books of such range and variety that there will be something to arouse the interest and further the learning of the dull and the bright, the practical and the theoretical, the poor reader, and the advanced student.

Studies have shown how closely good school libraries in elementary and secondary schools are related to academic achievement, to remaining in high school, and to going on to college. Project Talent, a research study covering almost half a million high school students, reports that the quality of the school library is, in fact, among the four most important factors closely associated with such measurements of student performance as staying in school, achievement, and going to college.

Yet despite a long-standing belief of educational leaders and the findings of research, literally thousands of public and nonpublic schools lacked libraries; literally millions of school pupils—especially elementary school pupils—did not have a school library available to them in the decades after the Second World War. Stated in terms of individual pupils, more than ten million pupils in public elementary, junior high and senior high schools—nearly 30 percent of all pupils over the nation—lacked access to a school library. The vast majority of these were in elementary schools—at the critical years for learning to read and developing a love of books and knowledge.

The situation, it has to be said, was similarly acute in colleges and universities, where the quality of instruction depended to a major degree on the quality and comprehensiveness of the library. Two percent of all academic libraries owned almost 39 percent of the volumes, spent 36 percent of total college outlays for library materials, and employed 35 percent of the total staff.

And the quality of public libraries throughout the nation varied sharply from region to region, as reflected in service, staffing, book collections, and financial support. Per capita funds for public libraries, for example, ranged from more than ten dollars per person in relatively wealthy communities to less than fifty cents per person in poor rural areas. Fully sixteen million people had no access to a local public library service. Books, in short, were not equally available to all students, and an equal quality of service was lacking. Many observers of the scene at mid-century were convinced that what had come to be called the "knowledge explosion" would require great strengthening of library resources and new methods of bringing the knowledge in books to the student.

Title II, in the 1965 Education Act, proposed to correct the inadequacies of teaching materials with a five-year program to make books and other printed materials available to the school children of the nation. Another program was adopted for the colleges. Library books, textbooks, periodicals, magnetic tapes, phonograph records, and other materials could be purchased with these funds. The decentralized system of education was reinforced by leaving to state and local educators decisions regarding the selection of books and other instructional materials. But there lay ahead the task of using these materials more efficiently and to better effect. Research and development programs could not pretend that the storing of knowledge or the present ways of making it available to those who wanted it were adequate. And finally there is the question of buildings. Will enough be built? In the right place? Projected increases in school enrollment suggest that the need for more schools and classrooms would if anything accelerate. In the decade after 1955, public school enrollments in kindergarten through the twelfth grade rose from 30.7 million to 42.1 million. Office of Education statisticians predicted that they would rise another 6 million by 1975, and still another 10 million by 1985.

Yet in spite of extraordinary efforts of state and local government some school systems lack the resources to provide all the necessary school sites, classrooms, and equipment. Outstanding bond indebtedness for school facilities increased from $4.5 billion in 1951–52 to $17.5 billion in 1961–62. Annual interest payments during this same period on school debt rose from $114 million to $588 million.

In the early 1960's a total of 351,000 public elementary and secondary classrooms were built. Of these, 227,000 were made necessary by increased enrollments. The other 124,000 replaced facilities worn out beyond use. Reports suggested that these 124,000 replacement classrooms did not appreciably decrease the number of off-site, nonpermanent, improvised, crowded, or unsafe classrooms. But enrollment increases are expected to be smaller in the following ten years than they were in the prior decade and the decrease may give school districts some breathing space to consider other construction needs, such as the replacement of obsolescent facilities. It is estimated that the number of classrooms built to accommodate increased enrollments will probably drop from the 227,000 constructed during the first five years of the decade to 112,000 for 1965–70, and to 95,000 in 1970–75. However, in 1964 the nation needed another 76,000 classrooms to eliminate the use of off-site or makeshift rooms. Another 98,000 were needed if the people wished to put all public school children in classes of 27.5 pupils or less.

Most nonpermanent classrooms—often unused military barracks

Table 17. Number of classrooms in backlog for the 50 states and the District of
Columbia, 1964–65

	Classrooms in backlog, 1965*	More desirable 25† elementary, 20 secondary)	Median (27.4 elementary, 27.5 secondary)	Less desirable (30 elementary, 30 secondary)
Overcrowding*		286,000	98,000	51,000
To replace:				
Makeshift	30,000	25,000	15,000	5,000
Non-permanent	31,000	25,000	15,000	5,000
Off-site	15,000	12,000	8,000	3,000
To replace: 4 or more defects	54,600	40,000	20,000	10,000
3 defects	104,000	90,000	40,000	20,000
Total		478,000	196,000	94,000
To be renovated and remodeled	230,000	230,000	100,000	50,000

NOTE: Median is a basic reference point and does not mean desirable. Does not include
outlying areas.

* *Condition of Public School Plants 1964–65*, George Collins and William Stormer,
Washington, D.C., Department of Health, Education, and Welfare, Office of Education, 1965.
George T. Collins, "School Building—Time to Slow Down?"; *School Management*, July,
1965, pp. 68–69.

† Pupils per room.

or similar wooden structures moved to the school site—were inadequate because of poor heating, poor lighting, and fire hazards. An
alternative was developed to overcome these functional deficiencies,
the mobile classroom. They can be safe, properly heated, and air-
conditioned. One major experiment with mobile classrooms, in Chicago, ran into severe and well-publicized trouble, but this was not
a function of the classrooms themselves, but rather of their alleged
use to continue *de facto* segregation. Mobile facilities showed promise
of help in providing educational spaces quickly in any location; an
important consideration to a population on the move. And on the
move the nation was and is likely to be. The Bureau of the Census

Table 18. Number of classrooms needed

	More desirable (25* elementary, 20 secondary)	Median (27.4 elementary, 27.5 secondary)	Less desirable (30 elementary, 30 secondary)
Enrollment increase	24,000	20,000	17,700
Migration	36,000	30,000	27,000
New program needs, 1965	10,000	7,500	3,000
Replace rooms abandoned and for consolidation	12,000	9,000	6,000
1965 total	82,000	66,500	53,700
1965–70 total	659,500	409,500	333,700
1965–75 total	1,184,500	739,500	567,700

NOTE: Median is a basic reference point and does not mean desirable. Annual construction rate has been about 70,000 rooms per year.
* Pupils per room.

reported that in recent years, 20 percent of the American people shifted homes annually—13 percent within a county, 7 percent from county to county. This means that about 12 percent of elementary and secondary students change schools each year—nearly 5 million out of a public school enrollment of about 41.5 million.

Tables 17 and 18 summarize the number of classrooms necessary to meet space requirements. Table 17 deals with the backlog; it takes no account of future enrollment increases, showing only how many classrooms are needed immediately to replace overcrowded or inadequate structures. Table 18 breaks down the 1965 demand to show the number of classrooms required to handle enrollment increases, migration, new programs, and the replacement of rooms abandoned in rural areas for consolidation in a more central location. In addition, Table 18 projects the 1965 demand into total figures for the next ten years.

The sheer size of the task is enough to call for research to find more efficient methods of design and construction. Another step clearly needed is to work out more efficient contracting methods by school systems which have not taken advantage of the economy of joint effort. Still another is the search for ways to place the schools in the community in order to help to solve problems of community growth, and racial and class tension.

One development—or, more accurately, hope—in school construction deserving further research was the educational park to permit all students in a community—from nursery school through community college—to attend classes at one center. Modifications of the plan included the possibility of sending all students above fifth grade to the educational park and retaining those in the lower grades in neighborhood schools. Proponents of the plan argued that it could be used to the end of integration of pupils from all races and all social and economic levels. Such integration seemed more likely to be accomplished through the educational park than by any other plan suggested, but the cost factors in the cities presented difficulties to educators and city officials alike so serious that many observers despaired of widespread use of the idea.

Besides building new schools, many administrators sought ways to increase the use of existing school facilities. Again, experiments had to be encouraged. By tradition, most schools shut down for more hours than they were open. They remained closed, on the average, from midafternoon until the following morning during the school term and throughout the day for about three months. Extending the use of schools through twelve months instead of the usual nine by summer programs was adopted by school systems in many parts of the country —though rarely as the basis of required attendance. Adult education and evening classes for high school students further stretched hard-pressed school budgets. But the problem of adequate financing for buildings had not been solved by the mid-1960's, nor had a method been developed to encourage, on an adequate scale, the exploration of new methods of construction or new methods of cooperative purchasing of materials. The largest item of cost among the instruments of learning had shown itself little susceptible to basic change.

And the review of these instruments of learning shows why Dean Sizer was right when he paired the probable influence of a vigorous entry into the field by the private sector with the new federal initiative. For these two forces could provide the major push toward the revolution in educational practices that lay ahead. The decentralized centers of management in both schools and colleges made it unlikely that they would be able by themselves to change their ways of proceeding, for they lacked the means either to finance research and development or to produce materials. Restraints placed on federal activity and control meant that there would be need of finding a way to use the results of federally financed research in the creation of new materials for learning, and to make them available to schools and colleges—and the obvious channel was by reform in the ways of both the public and the private sectors. Such reform was under way by the mid-1960's and promised to provide the driving power needed for the revolution in education demanded by the society.

IX   The Need for Leadership

The necessary revolution in American education, however, cannot
come about as a matter of course. The fact that it is necessary by no
means makes it inevitable. It will take farseeing and hardheaded
leadership.

But it is not always clear what leadership *is*. John W. Gardner, the
Secretary of the Department of Health, Education, and Welfare, wrote
in his former post as president of the Carnegie Corporation:

There are many different ways of leading, many kinds of leaders. Consider, for example, the marked contrasts between the politician and the
intellectual leader, the large-scale manager and the spiritual leader. One
sees solemn descriptions of the qualities needed for leadership without
any reference at all to the fact that the necessary attributes depend on
the kind of leadership under discussion. Even in a single field there may
be different kinds of leadership with different required attributes. Think
of the difference between the military hero and the military manager.

If social action is to occur, certain functions must be performed. The
problems facing the group or organization must be clarified, and ideas
necessary to their solution formulated. Objectives must be defined. There
must be widespread awareness of those objectives, and the will to achieve
them. Often those on whom action depends must develop new attitudes
and habits. Social machinery must be set in motion. . . .

But in the dispersed and fragmented power system that prevails in the
Nation as a whole one cannot say "So-and-so is powerful," without further
elaboration. Those who know how our system works always want to know,
"Powerful in what way? Powerful to accomplish what?" We have leaders

in business and leaders in government, military leaders and educational leaders, leaders in labor and in agriculture, leaders in science, in the world of art, and in many other special fields. As a rule, leaders in any one of these fields do not recognize the authority of leaders from a neighboring field. Often they don't even know one another, nor do they particularly want to. Mutual suspicion is just about as common as mutual respect—and a lot more common than mutual cooperation in manipulating society's levers.

In education there are many leaders and many different roles. These leaders view each other sometimes with respect, sometimes with a suspicion that makes difficult the achievement of their common goals. Nor is it clear what kind of educational leadership the society expects of its school superintendents, its school boards, its colleges of education, its universities, to say nothing of its state and federal officials.

Since the context of this book is the schools, and particularly some of the problems of the public schools, this chapter will deal with leadership in that area. And it will still further narrow its focus to the superintendency of schools, though it should be made clear at the outset that there are many other positions from which leadership has come and will emerge. Some of them have been discussed earlier: the scholars, the teachers, the publishing industry, the federal and state offices of education. But before embarking on a consideration of the superintendency, and in order to place the discussion in perspective, some consideration of the role of the great educational associations is needed.

The National Education Association, including its state subsidiaries and the specialized groups associated with it, has long played a major part in analyzing educational policy affecting the schools and in proposing solutions to some of their current problems. Its influence has been felt in state capitols as well as local school boards. The reports of the Educational Policies Commission form a record indispensable to the student of America's schools. Leaders who were elementary and high school principals, professors in colleges of education, and staff members of associations had more to do with the development of the junior high school movement and the "core" curriculum, for example, than did the superintendents. Their influence during the past four decades profoundly altered the priorities given to subjects taught. There are many observers, with whom the author agrees, who feel that such influence did not always work out for the best. The downgrading of attention on the teaching of language—both English and foreign—and on mathematics and science, which was the partial result of the efforts to achieve a core curriculum and a better program to teach for democracy, is a case in point. Few of those engaged in such efforts, of course, sought to reduce the quality of teaching in those subjects; in fact, they felt that their proposals would improve quality. In the end, judgment on what to do turned on the facts, and without adequate research, development, and experimentation, the facts were not available. Decisions had to be made by someone, however, either consciously or by default, and sooner or later the superintendent and the school board were involved. For the superintendent is the manager of the schools and the chief adviser to the school board. By his selection of staff and materials he inevitably sets curricular programs and teaching methods. His sense of policy and his estimate of the wise path to follow is the key to school development.

Leadership from educational associations and their members is not limited, of course, to curricular matters or school organization. Recent years have shown a rise in energy and power in organized teacher groups, affiliated either with the National Education Association or the American Federation of Teachers (AFL-CIO).

Superintendents and school boards had to grapple with collective bargaining, often with little experience or training in techniques of how to proceed. Aroused teacher groups also called for more voice in educational policy. The future will surely bring a change in the relations of teachers' organizations to the governing authorities of the schools, though few if any can predict confidently the form of the change itself. Only two factors seem clear: education must learn the techniques of negotiation and arbitration, and the states will become more important factors in the final decisions on salaries and working conditions. The superintendents, sharing their responsibilities with association and union leaders, have the opportunity to help to chart the new course.

There is another, more personal, reason for concentrating on the superintendency. The author for a number of years has worked with members of this lonely and harried profession. He has come to sympathize with their difficulties, has tried to help them in their labors, and has been a party to what they have done. In criticizing some of the weaknesses of recent years, as he does in the following pages, he is therefore criticizing himself as well. It seems more graceful to choose an area of leadership in which the opening words must be *mea culpa*.

Is the main job of school administration, it may be asked, primarily to improve the quality of what is taught and the effectiveness of teaching in the schools? To attempt anything else, many would say, is a diversion and a mistake: that job has not itself been well done, and as a result other groups of the society have had to take the lead. The public sometimes seems to rely more on other professions for advice on how to teach and what to teach than on the views of school administrators.

This state of affairs is the result not of too great an emphasis by school administrators on seemingly noneducational matters, but rather on a sometimes misplaced emphasis. For superintendents *have* been dealing with factors essential to any educational enterprise: the buildings, the budget, the salaries of the teachers. But by concentrating on these issues and devoting their energies to winning the necessary public support, some superintendents left out of account other and deeper social issues that would affect their pupils more profoundly. The profession of school administration may have been following the right policy but using inadequate means. In the short term, public approval based on an incomplete understanding of the issue involved may help to pass bond issues and keep things peaceful in town. But in the longer run, approval may turn into criticism if it develops in time that a building program is not dealing with the basic community issues effectively. Most basic economic or social problems cannot be handled by one "program" anyway. A complex of programs lasting many years is necessary. The lack of such programs designed to handle the shifting social composition of the schools of Northern cities is a case in point. By the time of the civil rights movement of the 1960's, the schools of the great cities had, in general, allowed themselves to become adjusted to *de facto* segregation rather than become a force for integration.

The root of the difficulty probably lies in an insufficient understanding of the nature of the problems involved. The school administrator who assesses the guidance problem as only one of advising pupils on what curriculum to take, or what jobs or colleges are available, seriously misunderstands the deeper issues both of national manpower and of the ways the pupil develops ideas on his own capacities and weaknesses. Good "public relations," which has demanded so much administrative attention in recent years because of the problems of expansion and of the need of raising salaries, may in the long run turn out to weaken the standing of educational administration as a respectable profession because it became an excuse for inaction on unpopular issues.

The difficulty is not simply that of the monkey and the gourd. It is subtler than that. For educational administration suffers from an almost crippling disability if compared to either medicine or law. It lacks either the hard, scientific evidence of medicine, or the precedent created by the well-established and formal means of the law, to bolster its arguments for educational policy. Favorable public support is a demonstrable fact, but many educational programs and ideas are purely speculative, with little basis on which to predict results. Educational results take a generation to measure, and the school board election is always just around the corner. Is it any wonder, then, with the pressing problems of expansion to face (and usually there is nothing speculative or uncertain about the numbers of children) that school administration has chosen to concentrate on quantitative rather than qualitative issues, where results are both speculative and uncertain?

If school administration turns its eyes toward influencing public policy in larger spheres than those of the local schools, it may have little to say, and may be accused of neglecting its main task. If it sticks to the local job, it will not know enough of the basic problems which the schools will be expected to help to solve, many of which are national in origin, and the result will be unsatisfactory even at the local level. There is evidence to suggest that this last situation has already come to pass. For surely one reason why there is grave concern over the dangers of federal control over education is that the public doubts the ability of local educational units either to resist pressures or to initiate programs. Possibly one of the reasons why the British plan of a balance of power between a centralized ministry of education and local school authorities works as well as it does is that the local authorities are held in relatively high esteem.

One of the characteristic factors affecting education in the American past and to a large extent today is that education seems to be everyone's business and no one's responsibility. In other areas of public concern, responsibilities are more clear. When a city faces an epidemic, public health officials and physicians decide what is needed and their decisions are promptly enforced. Fire departments agree on fire regulations, and police departments decide how to maintain public order. But in the field of education, associations of parents, citizens' organizations of various sorts and shapes, elected and appointed school boards and committees, and a host of vocal bystanders—all these disparate elements of American society have license to advise and prod (and sometimes bully) educators. The job of a hospital administrator or a prison warden evidently seems specialized enough to create public acquiescence to their decisions. In education, however, everyone regards himself as an authority. The schools are everyone's business.

This is by no means a bad thing, however irritating it may be to some educators. For it means that education is felt to be important, too important to be left to the educators alone. The public's concern for education is—or in any event can and should be—one of education's greatest strengths. Doubtless the spread in America of universal free and compulsory education, a dramatic revolution unmatched at the time by any other country, was due in large measure to public conviction that education was the people's right and therefore their responsibility. The schools have encouraged, even if they sometimes regretted, the participation of parents in the life of the school. The election of school boards by the public was considered a means of bringing the schools closer to the process of democracy. Educational leaders, no matter how elite and specialized a group they may have tried to be, or may become in the future, need to know the lay majority's concerns and anxieties, for they are educating that majority's children. The educational leadership in the United States cannot assume the position still widely held in Europe that the parents have nothing to say about their schools. Apart from the fact that this is dubious educational policy, for the parents *should* know what their children are studying, it is also an obviously stupid political policy in the United States.

Nevertheless, there are trends in education and in society itself that do not favor an enlightened, enlarged, and interested lay leadership.

The fact that the lay public is responsive to the problems of education does not necessarily mean that its response has always been relevant to the actual need, or, even if relevant, that it has always been effective.

Particularly in large urban centers today, parents are further and further removed from decision making in the government and in the management of their children's schools. Frustrated by forces they fear and do not understand, they may unite in boycotts or demonstrations, as in the parents and taxpayers' protests in New York City against the threatened loss of neighborhood schools and the growth of integration in some areas. Others who feel, on the contrary, that the school systems are moving too timidly to redress social injustice, have at times resorted to boycotts and other protests to register the opposite view. There have been sit-down strikes in the offices of mayors and boards of education, parades against policies of school committees, and demonstrations to demand the resignation (or to protest the resignation) of controversial school superintendents.

All of this indicates trouble. But it also indicates hope—for no one protests and boycotts who does not care. The fact is that the American people care deeply about education, a concern stimulated in recent years by the civil rights movement itself. And this concern can be transformed into strength. Only a revolution in educational quality can satisfy the demands of the public—and of the school leadership itself. But the problems of education are too technical to be resolved by political response to public demonstrations.

The official and legally constituted source of lay leadership has been the school board. How effective is this exercise of power? School boards have traditionally been elected—approximately 85 percent of them by popular vote, but, as America becomes more urbanized and neighborhood ties weaken, the shift may be away from elected and toward appointed school boards. On the average, the proportion of elected boards (as contrasted with appointed boards) varies inversely with size of district: the larger the district, the less likely it is to have an elected board. Aside from the exception that the appointive method is used in six Southern states (Georgia, Maryland, North Carolina, South Carolina, Tennessee, and Virginia) the concentration on appointed boards is to be found in large school districts scattered across the nation. Of 183 school districts with 20,000 or more pupils, more than one-fourth have appointed boards, and those forty-eight systems have more than four million pupils enrolled. Even in those areas that retain elected boards, school district consolidation has eliminated many of the smaller local units, so that board membership is drawn from an ever larger and looser constituency. The white leaders who formerly prevailed are now being challenged by the non-whites, as well as by other whites from other neighborhoods and former school districts where things were done in "different ways." The traditional patterns of control of education by lay leadership are shifting and new patterns are emerging. Whether the new is more effective than the old is a matter of debate.

For a number of years researchers have examined personal characteristics of board members (education, occupation, age, income, etc.) in attempts to see which selection method—election or appointment—attains the most competent members. Insofar as personal characteristics indicate competence, the assertion that one method is superior to the other has not been supported by research. In fact comparisons of elected and appointed board members reveal more similarities than differences.

Nonpartisanship as a criterion for leadership was claimed as an advantage for both selection methods. On the one hand, school board appointment is supposed to remove or relieve pressures that might be applied against board members if they had to run for office. According to this argument, a more representative body can be obtained if an elected official or body appoints the board. But that course also has its dangers, for the appointing authority can, if he has free rein, select those who reflect his views. It seems unrealistic to believe that elected appointing officials will always make selections on a nonpartisan basis, or that the removal of political labels will guarantee a nonpartisan election. Appointed members may feel obligated to their appointing agency, while elected members may feel obligated to the group that put them in office. Studies demonstrate what almost anyone would guess—that board members are not always disinterested public servants running for public office to discharge civic duty. Separate elections normally attract only a small number of voters, and it is possible to question whether an elected board is really representative of the community. Still, to overcome the limitations of both selection methods, some communities have established caucus committees, widely representative of the community, to screen candidates for office. To overcome the limited turnout of voters at special elections, certain school districts hold the school board election the same day as the general election and furnish nonpartisan ballots. Both appointed and elected members look to the power clique in their community for advice when important decisions are to be made.

The educational profession, in general, has supported the elective method, perhaps because this procedure divorces public education from control by the municipal government. (Most elected boards have fiscal independence.) By contrast, experts in public administration generally prefer appointed rather than elective boards, precisely because appointment brings the schools *closer* to the municipal government. (Most appointed boards are fiscally dependent.) These experts in administration feel that school financing should be considered from the standpoint of total community need, not as an isolated special service.

It is difficult to state with much assurance that one method of school board election is superior to the other. Both have produced superior, mediocre, and poor boards and leadership. But even within boards superior in quality of personnel, as with school administrators, the perspective of decision making may be narrow, based on immediate short-term goals that a longer view would alter. And it may in fact be true that more relationship to political goals rather than less would be desirable for the achievement of effective education—if political goals are seen, not in short-range terms such as patronage but in the long view of public policy.

H. Thomas James, professor of education at Stanford University, sees the problem as a matter not only of perspective but of temperament and disposition.

I believe there are good and sufficient reasons why the volume of policy made by boards of education is declining, and the volume made by legislatures (often at the initiative of the Congress) is increasing. Whether board members are directly elected or appointed by representatives of the people who are politically responsible to the electorate, they respond in most of the large cities to a tradition of being nonpolitical in the partisan sense. Thus, persons elected to boards of education rarely have occupied other political offices. The role of school board members is one of the last remaining opportunities in the political world for the "gentleman in public office." In many of the very large school systems, periods of relative peace and quiet in the management of the district's affairs have in the past been characterized by high incidence of "gentlemen." Fortunately or unfortunately, "gentleman in public office" have a marked distaste for controversy and public uproar, and will usually attempt to reduce conflict rather than extend it. Therefore, some of the most consequential educational issues of our time, because they have been the most violently controversial, have too often been sidestepped by boards of education, and so have had to be resolved in the less squeamish but more realistic arenas of partisan politics.

Such evasion of leadership has certainly been characteristic of many cities in the controversies of the sixties on civil rights. In other cities, however, school boards have been the *focus* of conflict. Failure to be involved politically may be a default of leadership; but involvement holds its dangers, too.

Students of government have commented on the important part played in the affairs of all levels of government by the representatives of organized special interests, popularly associated with lobbies and the application of direct political pressure for special and sometimes selfish purposes. As policy initiated by state legislature has increased, educational groups have tended to apply to the legislatures for succor. Teachers' groups bring pressure for better salaries and working conditions, arguing that reform is in the interest of the improvement of the quality of education for the children. To concentrate on this aspect of special interest groups, however, is to miss their role in uniting several levels of government with the private interests that have a stake in the issue at hand. Educators, through their associations, now have a strong voice in the lobbies of the state legislatures.

But how much direct responsibility does the public—as represented on school boards or in legislatures—have for the entire program of "public education"? Is it in charge of policy or have the superintendents assumed both operating and policy leadership? Or have lay boards taken on professional responsibilities better left to the educators themselves? On these issues there is continued and healthy debate.

Some school administrators have been under considerable criticism from those who charge that they have tended to follow rather than lead the attack upon certain crucial social and intellectual problems. It is argued that their actions have for the most part been in response to public pressure rather than the result of an effort to shape educational policy. Others are charged with taking too much on themselves.

It would be naïve to suggest that public pressure on policy makers is neither advisable nor effective. However, with the trend toward professional autonomy in education, and with the growing urgency of social problems, a clearer distinction between the public and professional domain in education is needed. The issues on which public pressure is exerted are far more important than the *amount* of pressure.

For administrators are moving into more and more exposed positions in which decisions affecting public policy cannot be avoided even if the administrator wished to avoid them. Superintendents and college presidents are standing on "the exposed front lines" (as they themselves describe it), catching the shards and shrapnel, while the rest of the education community, lay and professional, is relatively protected. Yet school administrators exist in part to allow teachers to teach without the constant bombardment of criticism from the society. The superintendency implies the role of leadership, and part of its function is to take responsibility both for the quality of instruction and for the relevance of the schools to the social issues of the day. School administrators often feel harassed by such demands; yet the demands have a positive side: they are increasing evidence of the seriousness of the public concern for education and of public realization that education is related to the total problems of the community.

Because of sheer numbers—more individual districts, more superintendents—the rural administrator used to be the spokesman for professional education, yet a shift toward urban leadership is coming swiftly and dramatically. Attention focuses today on the men who guide such school districts as New York, Los Angeles, Philadelphia, Chicago, Detroit, and Atlanta. Some manage budgets that exceed those of entire states, to say nothing of state departments of education. In these and other major urban centers, the superintendent of schools stands as prominently on the public stage as the mayor or city manager. Nor has this phenomenon of bigness been confined to cities alone: several states have elevated their county (or intermediate) school districts to top rank, with all the fiscal and political amenities that go with it. Annual salaries of $20,000 are commonplace for superintendents, and many are much higher. Over fifty of the top public school officials are paid more than $33,000 a year.

The trend toward larger units has its advantages. The more progressive among the nation's superintendents have become urban-minded and tend to prefer consolidation. They have fought for larger units in order to build school districts with a variety of instructional offerings: school orchestras, science fairs, vocational schools, adult education, radio and television, and well-stocked libraries.

But the very complexity of the task has created subdivision of authority and duty. Thus, instead of the single administrator carrying out the wishes of the lay leadership or boards, there may now be a school business official, a director of transportation, a food service manager, a buildings and grounds superintendent, a director of instructional personnel, a director of pupil personnel, a public relations coordinator, and many others. Some of these identify with taxpayer interests; others identify with the students or with the instructional staff, possibly in direct opposition to the taxpayer's concern with efficiency and thrift. The superintendent stands in the middle, and in large cities that has become an almost untenable position.

One might imagine this to be a time of great opportunity for the superintendent. Relieved of much of the daily administrative burden, with a panoply of subadministrators, he might have time and interest to exercise educational and community leadership. What does he have to say about segregated schools? Does he feel that public housing is being adequately planned? What is his stand on questions of academic freedom? How much and what type of in-service training does he think a teacher should be required to have? Does the community provide adequate health and welfare service to children?

On the average, he has found little time to lead in such matters. For the lay leadership has not fully understood that educational administration is not simply the job of being a school principal or headmaster on a larger scale. The change is one of kind, not of degree. The large city superintendent is a part of public administration, not a large-sized schoolmaster. Yet he is expected to be both at once—and there is not time nor the likelihood of one man being able to do both jobs equally well.

School administrators have customarily been victims of a kind of conflict between their role as professional specialists in education and their role as employees of the school system and the community. The distinction between public decisions and professional decisions has been hazy. Decisions reached cooperatively with the board of education on curriculum matters, for example, have usually been considered "better" because they were more democratically developed. Many school administrators, particularly in smaller units, have tended to pride themselves upon their responsibility for curriculum development and for strong participation by lay groups in the school program. But many had little real involvement with shaping public educational policy. Even within their own institutions they were frequently regarded as executive officers whose only responsibility was the execution of policies originated by the board of education.

The professional educator has his largest influence, without any question, however, in the local community. The administrative officers of the schools sit with the school committees in all their deliberations. Educators are customarily allowed a wide area of latitude in the implementation of policy. In many school systems the lay boards in practice have direct control only over matters of budget and building, while the curriculum and the quality of the teaching staff are relegated largely to the educational leadership. It is worth noting, in this connection, that a substantial change of curricular policy in both the elementary and the high school has taken place in the last half century, largely through the combined influence of the professional educators and special interest groups, with comparatively little public outcry or political activity. It is common for the teachers and administrators to be in close touch with the parents and the influential leaders of the smaller communities, and this control has therefore been exercised locally by them with relatively little friction, except in matters relating to the budget and to patronage in appointments or contracts.

After the Second World War, however, a variety of forces—international events, urban growth and decay, shifts in racial composition —have had a profound impact on metropolitan areas, and therefore on the schools that serve them. The evidence was available from political, economic, and sociological studies. But the graduate schools of education that prepare the administrators were slow. Graduate schools of educational administration on the average were slow to awaken to the change around them, and the superintendent who stumbles into a city riven by race riots and teacher union strikes or boycotts has had little academic preparation for such realities of his own profession. Even more significant was the lack of conscious attention to the relation of school policy to housing policy or welfare programs. The educational leader has not been ready to take his place on the team of public servants needed to bring about community change. He has tended to specialize, and in specializing to give his energy to tending to the machinery of his own area rather than exerting social and moral leadership. To quote Gardner again:

> But leadership, properly conceived, also serves the individual human goals that our society values so highly, and we shall not achieve goals without it.
>
> Leaders worthy of the name, whether they are university presidents or senators, corporation executives or newspaper editors, school superintendents or governors, contribute to the continuing definition and articulation of the most cherished values of our society. They offer, in short, moral leadership.
>
> So much of our energy has been devoted to tending the machinery of our complex society that we have neglected this element in leadership. I am using the word "moral" to refer to the shared values that must undergird any functioning society. The thing that makes a number of individuals a society rather than a population or a crowd is the presence of shared attitudes, habits and values, a shared conception of the enterprise of which they are all a part, shared views of why it is worthwhile for the enterprise to continue and to flourish. Leaders can help in bringing that about. In fact, it is required that they do so.

Taking his analysis as a guide, we may find it useful to see what the record of educational leadership has been. As we look back over the years since the end of the Second World War, what are the issues of public policy that have affected the schools, and on which the schools might be expected to have had an effect? Among them are: the population increase; inflation; the cold war; race relations; scientific progress and cultural advance; church and state relations; the relation of federal to state and local government; the allocation of resources; the problems of underdeveloped nations.

On how many of these matters has educational leadership taken a position of leadership in forming opinion and public policy? It appears to have taken the lead in the first two: educational effects of the population increase, and the effects of inflation on education. School administration as a professional field and school administrators as individuals have played a central part in proposing policies and persuading citizens and their local and state governments to handle a vast expansion of educational facilities. On balance, the record was good. Immense numbers of pupils were housed and hundreds of thousands of teachers employed. Salaries more than kept up with inflation. The American system of decentralization in educational management was put to a severe test, and did a far better job and in better style than many of its critics ever thought to be possible.

What about scientific progress and cultural advance? Did the profession take the lead in forming public policy on race relations? Does the public now place greater reliance than before on school administration to propose or to carry out new policies? Here the answer seems clearly to be "no." The nation established such bodies as the National Science Foundation to take initiative on reforms in education made necessary by scientific developments; and it has turned over to the judiciary and, more recently, to the executive arm of the federal government the powers of decision on policies in race relations. Individual school administrators have played a part, and often a very important part, in these developments. Consider, for example, the skillful work of John Fischer in school integration in Baltimore, in the 1950's, of Samuel Brownell in Detroit. But it cannot be said that the profession of school administration as a whole saw the problems coming, proposed policies or programs for their solution, and was assigned the major role in carrying out the task. School leaders did not in general take the lead in forming the necessary partnerships with economic leaders or housing authorities to try to change the social setting of the children they sought to teach. In general, educational leadership and their schools were forced into a position of reacting to outside pressure, rather than taking advantage of the pressures they had themselves helped to create. It can fairly be said that some basic educational decisions were being made in the 1950's and early 1960's by lawyers and scientists, not by the school administrators. Is leadership likely now to leave it to the lawyers to settle church-state issues, as though these did not involve profound educational problems requiring collaboration between public and private schools in carrying out the new education acts? Has school administration taken the lead in analyzing the various ways in which federal influence can be and should be exercised? Has educational administration felt a responsibility to take the lead in forming public policy in these matters?

The public image of the profession to many has been: Give us more money but do not tell us what to do with it. Recent years have not persuaded the American people that this is a sensible position to take. No profession deserves that much trust from the public. The issues are complex, not simple, and educational leadership should neither avoid them nor oversimplify them. It can be accused of both.

It may be that an analysis of the last two areas mentioned above— the allocation of resources and the problems of underdeveloped nations —will give a clue to why these statements have to be made. By and large, school administration since the Second World War has been fighting so hard to increase the allocation of *local* resources to education that it has not had time to consider the relation of education to the economy of the nation in broader terms. Concentration on money for schools per se, as if they were good in themselves and unrelated to the needs of the economy, has tended to obscure a fact which has become a fundamental aspect of modern society. As we have noted earlier, education should be thought of as investment directly related to greater productivity as well as a cost listed under the heading of consumption. Educational administration has not consciously conceived of itself as one aspect among many that go into making public policy on allocating resources for investment as well as consumption. Few references have been made in the profession to Professor Otto Eckstein's report on employment, growth, and price levels for the U.S. Joint Economic Committee of the Congress in 1959, which clearly connects investment in education with greater productivity. The tendency has been for school leaders to take for granted that education is a thing apart, to be detached from the issues of the day. For this reason, as professional men, most school administrators have tended to feel that the only aspect of public policy that falls within their ken is the allocation of money for schools.

Since he obtains most of his funds from local sources, it is inevitable that his eye is focused on the allocation of local resources. To the degree that his state allocates state resources to the schools, the school administrator considers the public policies of the state. So far he has relied on federal funds only for special purposes. One result of these conditions is that the role of investment in education as an aspect of economic policy has been obscured. The American economy is so complex that analysis by local or state categories is often meaningless. Only the over-all national picture can demonstrate that allocation of resources to education has the effect of increasing productivity.

Thus a consequence, though certainly an unintended one, of local control has been a local view of the school's relation to the economy. The school administrator has fought his battles for the tax dollar without one valuable ally—the economist—and against a foe—the local taxpayer—who can only see education as an expense and not as a source of ultimate increase in income.

A somewhat similar analysis of school administration in the political area might also be made. By deciding, perhaps wisely, that education on the local and state level should be kept free from political party alignments, school administration on the national scene has lost touch with the forces in society that initiate and control social reform. These forces are not necessarily political in the sense of being associated with a particular political party, but they work through political institutions. Earlier in this century, and in the last, education was always high on the list of the causes of the social reformers. It was an honorable member of the group who wanted to reform the civil service, big business, and child labor. Today the liberal and the social reformer want to reform education. Education is often seen as an entrenched self-interest. Educational leadership has often been forced to look on wistfully while its former friends eagerly plan a better world. Perhaps this was inevitable after the schools expanded to include all children, rich and poor, slow and quick. There was no longer reason for alliance with the liberals and reformers. But an equally good possibility is that educational leadership, by sticking close to the local job, by taking often a holier-than-thou attitude to other aspects of government, not only drifted away from its former friends, it also alienated them.

An example of this aloofness has been the role—or rather the lack of it—of school leadership in United States foreign policy toward underdeveloped nations. The economist and the political scientist have recently discovered, though it can scarcely be said to be a startling revelation, that an underdeveloped society must have a system of primary and secondary schools if its economy is to grow and its political goals are to be met. Investment in schools sensibly precedes or at least accompanies investment in steel mills. Yet there seems to be little evidence that school administration took the initiative in analyzing the problem or in bringing the weight of its opinion to bear. There were two reasons. The intellectuals who worried about such matters were not likely to have a good opinion of school leaders, whom they rather regarded as a kind of underdeveloped area at home, and were scarcely likely to seek their help. And school leadership saw little reason to be interested. Its job was local: its responsibilities did not include a role in foreign affairs, except to defend itself from time to time against the charge that some other country like England or Russia was doing a better job. Under these circumstances it is little wonder that school leadership has not played the part of law, of public health, of physics, or business in the formulation and execution of American foreign policy.

Obviously no single profession can be fully responsible for any aspect of national life; yet every profession has a part to play in many of our problems. As one looks deeply into our national problems, do not many of them have an educational side? If educational leadership is to mature, is it not its duty to enlarge its vision also?

The growing sense of responsibility among educators may at times conflict with the growing concern of the public. When that occurs, who is to lead? Are the people to follow in the wake of the educators, conceding the professionals' knowledge of curricula, teaching methods, and educational standards? Or must the educators wait for a consensus among the public before moving ahead? The answer to this apparent paradox is, of course, that both must lead. The stronger and more effective a school superintendent, the more likely he is to have public support. If his conception of his role proves too constricting and he evades decisions on urgent social issues—if, for example, he fails to do what he can to deal with *de facto* segregation and does not try to halt the exodus of white children from the public schools in his city—he cannot long survive as leader. If he is effective, a public consensus may grant him new authority. Educational issues always have taken and always will take their form partly from contemporary and political struggles.

Policy on debated educational issues should be worked out by educational leaders, but with the understanding that they need fresh ideas from outside their own ranks. Some of the best reforms in American education have come about because allies from the general public emerged at a critical point to support embattled educators. Top scientists have helped to remake the physics curriculum, and men like James B. Conant have stimulated the revitalization of teacher training. Not "educators" in the most narrow and formal sense of the word, they were drawn into the fray in part because of the leadership void among the educators. But hoping that a vacuum will draw in the right kind of help from the outside is scarcely an adequate approach to educational strategy.

If educational leaders had a set of strong educational and social views, views stemming from their common task as school administrators, they would at least have allies in their own profession, as other professionals have in theirs. But with allies or not, educational leaders have long ago learned that they will often wind up in a fight. Leadership has to decide on which ground to take its stand. As it must in every walk of life, from time to time leadership must be prepared to put its jobs on the line.

American educators have to be sensitive, of course, to the needs and concerns of the parents who pay for their schools. But if those needs and concerns conflict with the wider needs of society, then the leader's task is to find a resolution or to resign. The lack of either action may lead, if it has not already, to loss of power to influence public thinking on education before trouble starts. Educational leadership cannot walk alone. The great challenge for the future is to reorganize education into a more responsive and responsible governmental unit, able to deal effectively with other governmental units— which are, of course, also undergoing change and feeling out the limits of their power.

There are hopeful signs of new developments, both in the minds of individual superintendents and in their association, the American

Association of School Administrators. The change in the agenda of the topics at their annual meeting in Atlantic City between 1963 and 1966 is a dramatic example: scarcely a controversial issue was omitted in the latter year, and few could be found in the former. And in 1966, Wendell H. Pierce of Cincinnati dealt directly in a major address with the problems of the new federal-state-local partnership:

This new era of partnership is going to require some shifting of roles, some new understandings and certain new objectives. In some areas this is going to be difficult because antagonisms and suspicions have developed through the long effort to establish a federal-aid program and our failure to resolve the conflict regarding philosophy of purposes and forms of such aid. There are persons with public voices who desire a national system of education . . . and there are citizens, particularly educators, who cannot resolve the issue of categorical versus general aid programs. The superintendent, therefore, must assume responsibility for thinking through this question and determining his specific role in its resolution.

Second, each of us must evidence a mutuality of interest in the best education for all children, recognizing the part that each level of government must contribute. Strong state departments of education must be in the vanguard of the effort to implement quality education for all children, and superintendents must give every assistance to the state departments of education in the fulfillment of this role.

Third, we must join forces to work for better legislation at both the state and national level. It is for this reason that I see the strength of the Compact for Education, now being developed by the several states under the leadership of former Governor Terry Sanford and many state governors. While I recognize that there are problems in an intimate working relationship between educators and politicians, my own personal experience leads me to believe that politicians have a much better understanding of the problems of education than we credit them with. In the long run, a more intimate working relationship will make it possible to develop a much sounder legislative program at the state and national levels than can be accomplished by educators attempting to achieve the same goal independently.

Fourth, for the sake of this new partnership, we must be prepared to permit each other some mistakes and some margin of error. Those of us with experience in education recognize that all human beings do make mistakes and are subject to error. Most school administrators have suffered the experience of having a subordinate make a mistake and have had to come to the support of that individual. Also, most of us have learned that there is educational value in mistakes; that a part of growing up is in helping the other person learn how to profit from mistakes and to make fewer of them in the future. This same approach, it seems to me, is applicable as we attempt to work with our new partner, the federal government.

Yet the public cannot expect miracles of one man or of an entire school board or the educational leadership as a whole. If public expectations are high, the public must grant its educators power to realize those expectations. Public and private organizations must be ready with organized support when administrators and school boards need it. Lay leadership and school leadership; local, state, and federal leadership; industrial and private leadership—each will have to understand the problems of the other if education is to change at the rate and in the way the future seems to require.

Schools do not operate in a vacuum. In city and state and federal governments, leadership has not grappled adequately with the relation of the schools to housing, welfare, or urban redevelopment. The school superintendent is involved, whether he likes it or not, in social change. The schools are the social order, and if they change themselves, they inevitably change the order. Educational leadership is caught between Scylla and Charybdis. Because they cannot solve the problems of the total community by themselves, some leaders have reached the wrong conclusion that it is, therefore, not their responsibility to take initiative at all. The fact that they do not themselves have the means to solve society's major problems does not imply that they do not have any responsibility toward the solution of those problems.

The central problems facing school leadership lie in four areas: (a) in its relation to economic and political developments; (b) in the restrictions on thinking and planning caused by the American pattern of local control; (c) in the tendency to rely on current public opinion rather than long-term solutions to public issues; and (d) in the lack of dependable evidence on which to predict the results of educational programs.

These statements suggest that school administration might devote its energies to the analysis of its training programs, to its professional association, and to the need for research and development. If it be true that education is inextricably linked with economic and political development, both in developed and underdeveloped economies, then it is true that school administration is linked to public administration. One might even consider it an aspect of the larger field of scholarly work and professional training called by that name. It suggests that the analysis of political and economic problems must be central to the training of the school leader. One may even speculate on the possibility that economic support for schools, urban redevelopment, and race relations might take a different form today had school administration in past years been based on intensive studies in history, economics, political science, and sociology.

This country has paid a heavy price for the separation of school administration from public administration. Members of the profession should be trained to think as public servants whose special application is to be in education, rather than as administrators whose only concern is the schools. An administrator class should not be trained merely in process, but also in the ends to be served. The roots of educational thinking into political philosophy, economics, and history need to be deepened, accompanied by an analysis of the relation of these studies to the curricula of the schools. Education in the next fifty years must not be left out in the councils of state, as it has been so often in the last fifty years.

Men who see their problems in the broader terms that will come from study in history and economics, political science, philosophy, and sociology will not be bound by the parochialism of thought that is the danger of local control. Their interest in the curriculum will flow from their interest in public issues, and their view of what education can do in meeting these issues will be guided by their knowledge of the curriculum. We may be able to avoid the rather wild swings of the pendulum that we have seen in recent years in the sciences and the arts. But this will require more than training alone, of course. The profession of school administration will have to develop a more self-conscious attitude toward its role in helping to formulate public policy. The American Association of School Administrators, by its part in the Educational Policies Commission, has for many years been active in proposing policies for the schools. Yet it has not been the stimulating force that it might have been if its membership had joined in the analysis of the tougher issues of public policy.

If changes in training are the first steps, then changes in the climate of thought of professional associations are the second. The two, of course, are related, and cooperation between the profession and the universities is essential.

School administration can become, if it will, a profession whose voice can help to guide national decisions in matters of public policy. Not that school administration should be the final arbiter on educational matters, for it suffers from the same weakness as the military or medicine or any other professional field and should of course be checked by the regular processes of our form of government. To serve as a guide, it must have a deeper understanding than it now has of the economic, social, and political factors that underlie the great issues of our time. This means prior training, constant analysis, and a vigorous program of research and development. It means also the willingness, indeed the sense of duty, to see education in its context and propose policies and programs even though these may not at the moment be in the public fashion and may indeed not be agreed to by all members of the profession itself. Such action by professional groups in education, to put it delicately, is not common. As a result there is a marked trend in the public to regard any professional group in education as primarily concerned with its own, not the public, welfare. Its advice is therefore discounted.

To reverse this trend requires at least three steps:

1. The superintendency must first see itself in a new light. In addition to its present self-conception as the executive servant of the local board of education, the leader of the teaching staff, and the professional adviser to the local board, it must feel a corporate sense of responsibility as a professional adviser on issues of public policy that affect education and on which education has an effect. Rather than make more difficult the present role conflicts of the school administrator in his local community, such a change will make his local task easier. He will be seen

as a participant in a larger movement, as a man of standing in a larger community. The development of public confidence in the professional capacity of the school leader is a necessary step in solving the problem of federal versus local control of education.

2. Educational administration, having reached this self-view, must relate itself to other aspects of public administration, and particularly to economic policy, programs of social reform, and foreign affairs. One can imagine a pattern of analysis and influence comparable to that of the Committee on Economic Development, representative of progressive business administration, which in 1960 proposed policies on *Guiding Metropolitan Growth, Paying for Better Public Schools and National Objectives and the Balance of Payments Problem.* These reports were carefully prepared and had substantial influence on the thinking of both government and private groups. Surely the same road is open to school leadership.

3. After having taken these two steps, school administration would be ready to become an active participant in the formulation and execution of national policy. Its statements would be heeded in the halls of Congress, in the executive branch of the government, and in the judiciary. Even the fourth estate might be impressed.

As John Gardner put it:

The cure is not to work against the fragmentation of leadership, which is a vital element in our pluralism, but to create better channels of communication among significant leadership groups, especially in connection with the great issues that transcend any particular group.

What has been said so far about school leadership could of course be adapted for leadership in higher education, in professional or scholarly associations, and in every aspect of our complex educational enterprise. For when schools or colleges fail, the heart of the community decays—and that is the concern of businessmen, of clergymen, of politicians, and of parents—not just the concern of professional educators alone. A beleaguered superintendent may find a post somewhere else, but factories, stores, churches, and homes are rooted in one place. So are the people who work, worship, and live in them. No city in a great democracy can survive without education. Citizens who guard their schools guard their own future, and their best guardian is a leadership able to cultivate the common goals, the shared attitudes and values. "When leaders lose their credibility or their moral authority," Gardner wrote, "then the society begins to disintegrate."

So we end as we began. What Jaeger said about Greek culture and education can equally be applied to the Great Society of the United States in the twentieth century: the basis of education is a general consciousness of the values which govern human life. Leadership's task is to state these values and to interpret them. American education, that great engine of the democracy, does not drive itself. It must be guided, not by one but by many, into a future of incalculable promise.

Appendix A]

Message on Education from
the President of the United States

88th Congress, 1st Session
To the Congress of the United States:

Education is the keystone in the arch of freedom and progress. Nothing has contributed more to the enlargement of this Nation's strength and opportunities than our traditional system of free, universal elementary and secondary education, coupled with widespread availability of college education.

For the individual, the doors to the schoolhouse, to the library and to the college lead to the richest treasures of our open society: to the power of knowledge—to the training and skills necessary for productive employment—to the wisdom, the ideals, and the culture which enrich life—and to the creative, self-disciplined understanding of society needed for good citizenship in today's changing and challenging world.

For the Nation, increasing the quality and availability of education is vital to both our national security and our domestic well-being. A free nation can rise no higher than the standard of excellence set in its schools and colleges. Ignorance and illiteracy, unskilled workers and school dropouts—these and other failures of our educational system breed failures in our social and economic system: delinquency, unemployment, chronic dependence, a waste of human resources, a loss of productive power and purchasing power and an increase in tax-supported benefits. The loss of only 1 year's income due to unemployment is more than the total cost of 12 years of education through high school. Failure to improve educational performance is thus not only poor social policy, it is poor economics.

At the turn of the century, only 10 percent of our adults had a high school or college education. Today such an education has become a requirement for an increasing number of jobs. Yet nearly 40 percent of our youths are dropping out before graduating from high school; only 43 percent of our adults have completed high school; only 8 percent of our adults have completed college; and only 16 percent of our young people are presently completing college. As my Science Advisory Committee has reported, one of our most serious manpower shortages is the lack of Ph.D's in engineering, science, and mathematics; only about one-half of 1 percent of our school-age generation is achieving Ph.D. degrees in all fields.

This Nation is committed to greater investment in economic growth; and recent research has shown that one of the most beneficial of all such investments is education, accounting for some 40 percent of the Nation's growth and productivity in recent years. It is an investment which yields a substantial return in the higher wages and purchasing power of trained workers, in the new products and techniques which come from skilled minds and in the constant expansion of this Nation's storehouse of useful knowledge.

In the new age of science and space, improved education is essential to give new meaning to our national purpose and power. In the last 20 years, mankind has acquired more scientific information than in all of previous history. Ninety percent of all the scientists that ever lived are alive and working today. Vast stretches of the unknown are being explored every day for military, medical, commercial and other reasons. And finally, the twisting course of the cold war requires a citizenry that understands our principles and problems. It requires skilled manpower and brainpower to match the power of totalitarian discipline. It requires a scientific effort which demonstrates the superiority of freedom. And it requires an electorate in every State with sufficiently broad horizons and sufficient maturity of judgment to guide this Nation safely through whatever lies ahead.

In short, from every point of view, education is of paramount concern to the national interest as well as to each individual. Today we need a new standard of excellence in education, matched by the fullest possible access to educational opportunities, enabling each citizen to develop his talents to the maximum possible extent.

Our concern as a Nation for the future of our children—and the growing demands of modern education which Federal financing is better able to assist—make it necessary to expand Federal aid to education beyond the existing limited number of special programs. We can no longer afford the luxury of endless debate over all the complicated and sensitive questions raised by each new proposal on Federal participation in education. To be sure, these are all hard problems—but this Nation has not come to its present position of leadership by avoiding hard problems. We are at a point in history when we must face and resolve these problems.

State and local governments and private institutions, responsive to individual and local circumstances, have admirably served larger national purposes as well. They have written a remarkable record of freedom of thought and independence of judgment; and they have, in recent years, devoted sharply increased resources to education. Total national outlays for education nearly trebled during the 1940's and more than doubled during the 1950's, reaching a level of nearly $25 billion in 1960. As a proportion of national income, this represented a rise from little more than 4 percent in 1940 to nearly 6 percent in 1960, an increase in over 40 percent in total effort.

But all this has not been enough. And the Federal Government—despite increasing recognition of education as a nationwide challenge, and despite the increased financial difficulties encountered by States, communities, and private institutions in carrying this burden—has clearly not met its responsibilities in education. It has not offered sufficient help to our present educational system to meet its inadequacies and overcome its obstacles.

I do not say that the Federal Government should take over responsibility for education. That is neither desirable nor feasible. Instead its participation should be selective, stimulative and, where possible, transitional.

A century of experience with land-grant colleges has demonstrated that Federal financial participation can assist educational progress and growth without Federal control. In the last decade, experience with the National Science Foundation, with the National Defense Education Act, and with programs for assisting federally affected school districts has demonstrated that Federal support can benefit education without leading to Federal control. The proper Federal role is to identify national education goals and to help local, State, and private authorities build the necessary roads to reach those goals. Federal aid will enable our schools, colleges and universities to be more stable financially and therefore more independent.

These goals include the following:

First, we must improve the *quality* of instruction provided in all of our schools and colleges. We must stimulate interest in learning in order to reduce the alarming number of students who now drop out of school or who do not continue into higher levels of education. This requires more and better teachers—teachers who can be attracted to and retained in schools and colleges only if pay levels reflect more adequately the value of the services they render. It also requires that our teachers and instructors be equipped with the best possible teaching materials and curriculums. They must have at their command methods of instruction proven by thorough scientific research into the learning process and by careful experimentation.

Second, our educational system faces a major problem of *quantity*—of coping with the needs of our expanding population and of the rising educational expectations for our children which all of us share as parents. Nearly 50 million people were enrolled in our schools and colleges in 1962—an increase of more than 50 percent since 1950. By 1970, college enrollment will nearly double, and secondary schools will increase enrollment by 50 percent—categories in which the cost of education, including facilities, is several times higher than in elementary schools.

Third, we must give special attention to increasing the *opportunities* and *incentives* for all Americans to develop their talents to the utmost— to complete their education and to continue their self-development throughout life. This means preventing school dropouts, improving and expanding special educational services, and providing better education in slum, distressed and rural areas where the educational attainment of students is far below par. It means increased opportunities for those students both willing and intellectually able to advance their education at the college and graduate levels. It means increased attention to vocational and technical education, which have long been underdeveloped in both effectiveness and scope, to the detriment of our workers and our technological progress.

In support of these three basic goals, I am proposing today a comprehensive, balanced program to enlarge the Federal Government's investment in the education of its citizens—a program aimed at increasing the educational opportunities of potentially every American citizen, regardless of age, race, religion, income, and educational achievement.

This program has been shaped to meet our goals on the basis of three fundamental guidelines:

(*a*) An appraisal of the entire range of educational problems, viewing educational opportunity as a continuous lifelong process, starting with preschool training and extending through elementary and secondary schools, college, graduate education, vocational education, job training and retraining adult education, and such general community educational resources as the public library;

(*b*) A selective application of Federal aid—aimed at strengthening, not weakening, the independence of existing school systems and aimed at meeting our most urgent education problems and objectives, including quality improvement; teacher training; special problems of slum, depressed, and rural areas; needy students; manpower shortage areas such as science and engineering; and shortages of educational facilities; and

(*c*) More effective implementation of existing laws, as reflected in my recent budget recommendations.

To enable the full range of educational needs to be considered as a whole, I am transmitting to the Congress with this message a single, comprehensive education bill—the National Education Improvement Act of 1963. For education cannot easily or wisely be divided into separate parts. Each part is linked to the other. The colleges depend on the work of the schools; the schools depend on the colleges for teachers; vocational and technical education is not separate from general education. This bill recalls the posture of Jefferson: "Nobody can doubt my zeal for the general instruction of the people. I never have proposed a sacrifice of the primary to the ultimate grade of instruction. Let us keep our eye steadily on the whole system."

In order that its full relation to economic growth, to the new age of science, to the national security, and to human and institutional freedom may be analyzed in proper perspective, this bill should be considered as a whole, as a combination of elements designed to solve problems that have no single solution.

This is not a partisan measure—and it neither includes nor rejects all of the features which have long been sought by the various educational groups and organizations. It is instead an attempt to launch a prudent and balanced program drawing upon the efforts of many past Congresses and the proposals and many Members of both Houses and both political parties. It is solely an educational program, without trying to solve all other difficult domestic problems. It is clearly realistic in terms of its cost—and it is clearly essential to the growth and security of this country.

I. THE EXPANSION OF OPPORTUNITIES FOR INDIVIDUALS IN HIGHER EDUCATION

Our present American educational system was founded on the principle that opportunity for education in this country should be available to all—not merely to those who have the ability to pay. In the past, this has meant free public elementary and secondary schools in every community—thereafter, land-grant, State, and municipal colleges, and vocational education—and more recently, job retraining and specialized teachers for students with special educational problems.

Now a veritable tidal wave of students is advancing inexorably on our institutions of higher education, where the annual costs per student are several times as high as the cost of a high school education, and where these costs must be borne in large part by the student or his parents. Five years ago the graduating class of the secondary schools was 1.5 million; 5 years from now it will be 2.5 million. The future of these young people and the Nation rests in large part on their access to college and graduate education. For this country reserves its highest honors for only one kind of aristocracy—that which the Founding Fathers called "an aristocracy of achievement arising out of a democracy of opportunity."

Well over half of all parents with school-age children expect them to attend college. But only one-third do so. Some 40 percent of those who enter college do not graduate, and only a small number continue into graduate and professional study. The lack of adequate aid to students plays a large part in this disturbing record.

Federal aid to college students is not new. More than 3 million World War II and Korean conflict veterans have received $6 billion in Federal funds since 1944 to assist them to attend college.

Additionally, the National Defense Education Act college student loan program has aided more than 300,000 students in more than 1,500 institutions who have borrowed nearly $220 million. In 4 years of operations, defaults have totaled only $700 while repayment rates are more than twice that required by law.

But as effective as this program has been, it has not fulfilled its original objective of assuring that "no student of ability will be denied an opportunity for higher education because of financial need." The institutional ceiling of $250,000 per year on the Federal contribution limits loan funds in at least 98 of the presently participating institutions. The annual statutory ceiling of $90 million on Federal appropriations restricts the size of the program. As a result, only about 5 percent of the students enrolled in participating colleges are assisted. Additionally, the forgiveness feature for teachers is rendered less attractive as well as less meaningful by excluding those who go on to teach in colleges, private schools, or on overseas military posts. This proven program must be enlarged and strengthened.

Other types of assistance are needed. For students who cannot meet the financial criteria under the National Defense Education Act loan program, a loan insurance program—drawing on techniques well established by the FHA and other Federal programs—would encourage banks and other institutions to loan more money for educational purposes.

Moreover, many students from families with limited incomes cannot and should not carry a heavy burden of debt. They must rely largely on income from employment while in college. For these students, the Federal Government should—as it did in the days of the National Youth Administration—help colleges provide additional student work opportunities of an educational character.

A serious barrier to increased graduate study is the lack of adequate financial aid for graduate students. Only 1,500 fellowships are permitted annually under the National Defense Education Act program, upon which we are dependent for urgently needed increases in the number of college teachers and the number of graduate students pursuing other courses essential to the Nation's advancement and security. The National Science Foundation has broad authority for fellowships and training grants, but its program, too, has been restricted by limited appropriations. The President's Science Advisory Committee has predicted that the dramatically increasing demand for engineers, mathematicians, and physical scientists, will require that the output of Ph.D.'s in these fields alone be increased 2½ times, to a total of 7,500 annually by 1970, and that the number of master's degrees awarded annually be substantially increased. In all fields the need exceeds the supply of doctoral recipients. The shortage is particularly acute in college teaching, where at present rates the Nation will lack 90,000 doctoral degree holders by 1970. It is clearly contrary to the national interest to have the number of graduate students limited by the financial ability of those able and interested in pursuing advanced degrees. Fellowship programs can ease much of the financial burden and, most importantly, encourage and stimulate a fuller realization and utilization of our human resources.

The welfare and security of the Nation require that we increase our investment in financial assistance for college students both at undergraduate and graduate levels. In keeping with present needs and our traditions of maximum self-help, *I recommend that the Congress enact legislation to—*

1. Extend the National Defense Education Act student loan program, liberalize the repayment forgiveness for teachers, raise the ceiling on total appropriations and eliminate the limitation on amounts available to individual institutions.

2. Authorize a supplementary new program of Federal insurance for commercial loans made by banks and other institutions to college students for educational purposes.

3. Establish a new work-study program for needy college students unable to carry too heavy a loan burden, providing up to half the pay for students employed by the colleges in work of an educational character—as, for example, laboratory, library, or research assistants.

4. Increase the number of National Defense Education Act fellowships to be awarded by the Office of Education from 1,500 to 12,000, including summer session awards.

5. Authorize a thorough survey and evaluation of the need for scholarships or additional financial assistance to undergraduate students so that any further action needed in this area can be considered by the next Congress.

6. In addition, as part of this program to increase financial assistance to students, the 1964 budget recommendations for the National Science Foundation, which are already before the Congress, include a proposed increase of $35 million to expand the number of fellowships and new teaching grants for graduate study from 2,800 in 1963 to 8,700 in fiscal 1964.

II. EXPANSION AND IMPROVEMENT OF HIGHER EDUCATION

Aid to college students will be to no avail if there are insufficient college classrooms. The long-predicted crisis in higher education facilities is now at hand. For the next 15 years, even without additional student aid, enrollment increases in colleges will average 340,000 each year. If we are to accommodate the projected enrollment of more than 7 million college students by 1970—a doubling during the decade—$23 billion of new facilities will be needed, more than three times the quantity built during the preceding decade. This means that, unless we are to deny higher education opportunities to our youth, American colleges and universities must expand their academic facilities at a rate much faster than their present resources will permit.

In many colleges, students with adequate modern dormitories and living quarters—thanks to the College Housing Act—are crammed in outmoded, overcrowded classrooms, laboratories, and libraries. Even now it is too late to provide these facilities to meet the sharp increases in college enrollment expected during the next 2 years. Further delay will aggravate an already critical situation.

I recommend, therefore, the prompt enactment of a program to provide loans to public and nonprofit private institutions of higher education for construction of urgently needed academic facilities.

The opportunity for a college education is severely limited for hundreds of thousands of young people because there is no college in their own community. Studies indicate that the likelihood of going to college on the part of a high school graduate who lives within 20 to 25 miles of a college is 50-percent greater than it is for the student who lives beyond commuting distance. This absence of college facilities in many communities causes an unfortunate waste of some of our most promising youthful talent. A demonstrated method of meeting this particular problem effectively is the creation of 2-year community colleges—a program that should be undertaken without delay and which will require Federal assistance for the construction of adequate facilities.

I recommend, therefore, a program of grants to States for construction of public community junior colleges.

There is an especially urgent need for college-level training of technicians to assist scientists, engineers, and doctors. Although ideally one scientist or engineer should have the backing of two or three technicians, our institutions today are not producing even one technician for each three science and engineering graduates. This shortage results in an inefficient use of professional manpower—the occupation of critically needed time and talent to perform tasks which could be performed by others—an extravagance which cannot be tolerated when the Nation's demand for scientists, engineers, and doctors continues to grow. Failure to give attention to this matter will impede the objectives of the graduate and postgraduate training programs mentioned below.

I recommend, therefore, a program of grants to aid public and private nonprofit institutions in the training of scientific, engineering, and medical technicians in 2-year, college-level programs, covering up to 50 percent of the cost of constructing and equipping as well as operating the necessary academic facilities.

Special urgency exists for expanding the capacity for the graduate training of engineers, scientists, and mathematicians. The President's Science Advisory Committee has recently reported that an unprecedented acceleration in the production of advanced degrees is immediately necessary to increase our national capability in these fields. Added facilities, larger faculties, and new institutions are needed. *I have recommended, therefore, in the proposed 1964 budget already before the Congress, a strengthening of the National Science Foundation matching-grant program for institutions of higher education to expand and improve graduate and undergraduate science facilities.*

Because today's trend in colleges and universities is toward less lecturing and more independent study, the college and university library becomes even more essential in the life of our students. Today, as reported by the American Library Association, nearly all college libraries are urgently in need of additional books, periodicals, scientific reports and similar materials to accommodate the growing number of students and faculty. Additionally, they need buildings, equipment, and publications to serve their academic communities, whether public or private.

I recommend the authorization of Federal grants to institutions of higher education for library materials and construction, on a broad geographic basis, with priority to those most urgently requiring expansion and improvement.

Expansion of high quality graduate education and research in all fields is essential to national security and economic growth. Means of increasing our supply of highly trained professional personnel to match the rapidly growing demands of teaching, industry, government, and research warrants our interest and support.

We need many more graduate centers, and they should be better distributed geographically. Three-quarters of all doctoral degrees are granted by a handful of universities located in 12 States. The remaining States with half our population produce only one-fourth of the Ph.D.'s.

New industries increasingly gravitate to or are innovated by strong centers of learning and research. The distressed area of the future may well be one which lacks centers of graduate education and research. It is in the national interest to encourage establishment of these critically needed centers of advanced learning, especially in parts of the Nation now lacking them.

I recommend enactment of a Federal grant program administered by the Department of Health, Education, and Welfare for the development and expansion of new graduate centers. I also urge appropriation of the increased funds requested in my 1964 budget for expansion of the National Science Foundation program of science development grants, which will also contribute to strengthening of graduate education.

Our experience under the National Defense Education Act with respect to modern language and area centers has demonstrated that Federal aid can spur development of intellectual talent. They deserve our continuing support, with assurance that resources will be available for orderly expansion in keeping with availability of teaching talent.

I recommend that the current modern foreign language program aiding public and private institutions of higher learning be extended and expanded.

III. IMPROVEMENT OF EDUCATIONAL QUALITY

A basic source of knowledge is research. Industry has long realized this truth. Health and agriculture have established the worth of systematic research and development. But research in education has been astonishingly meager and frequently ignored. A fraction of 1 percent of this Nation's total expenditures for education is now devoted to such research. It is appalling that so little is known about the level of performance, comparative value of alternative investment and specialized problems of our educational system—and that it lags behind, sometimes by as much as 20 or even 50 years, in utilizing the result of research and keeping abreast of man's knowledge in all fields, including education itself.

Highest priority must be given to strengthening our educational research efforts, including a substantial expansion of the course content improvement programs which the Government has supported, particularly through the National Science Foundation. Two interrelated actions are necessary:

1. I have recommended appropriations in the 1964 budget for substantially expanding the National Science Foundation science and mathematics course materials program and the Office of Education educational research program.

2. I recommend legislation to broaden the Cooperative Research Act to authorize support of centers for multipurpose educational research, and for development and demonstration programs; and to broaden the types of educational agencies eligible to conduct research.

The second step to improvement of educational quality is *teacher training*. The quality of education is determined primarily by the quality of the teacher. Yet one out of every five teachers in the United States has either not been certified by his State as qualified to teach or failed to complete 4 years of college study. In the field of English, between 40 and 60 percent of the secondary school teachers lack even the minimum requirement of a college major in that subject. Thus it is not surprising that, largely because of unsatisfactory elementary and secondary school instruction, our colleges and universities are now required to spend over $10 million annually on remedial English courses.

The lack of teacher quality and preparation in other fields is equally disturbing. More than two-thirds of our 1.6 million teachers completed their degree work more than 5 years ago. Yet, within the past 5 years, major advances have been made—not only in the physical, biological, engineering, and mathematical sciences, but also in specialized branches of the social sciences, the arts and humanities, and in the art of teaching itself.

In addition, we lack sufficient trained teachers for 6 million handicapped children and youth, including 1.5 million mentally retarded and another 1.5 million with very serious social and emotional problems. Only through special classes, taught by specially trained teachers, can these children prepare for rehabilitation, employment, and community participation. Yet less than one-fourth of these children now have access to the special education they require, primarily because of the lack of qualified special teachers, college instructors, research personnel, and supervisors. It is estimated that 75,000 special teachers—55,000 more than presently available—are needed for the mentally retarded alone.

The teacher training support programs of the National Science Foundation and the Office of Education have demonstrated their value.

I recommend, therefore—

That the National Science Foundation program for training institutes for teachers in the natural sciences, mathematics, engineering, and social sciences be expanded to provide for upgrading the knowledge and skills of 46,000 teachers, as provided in my 1964 budget recommendations.

That new legislation be enacted to (a) broaden authority for teacher institutes financed by the Office of Education, now restricted to school guidance counselors and language teachers, to other academic fields; (b) authorize a program of project grants to help colleges and universities improve their teacher preparation programs by upgrading academic courses and staff, by encouraging the selection and retention of their most talented prospective teachers, and by attracting and training teachers from new sources such as retired military personnel or women whose family responsibilities permit them to teach, and (c) authorize training grants through colleges and universities for teachers and other education personnel requiring specialized training, with particular emphasis on the training of teachers of the mentally retarded and other handicapped children, teachers of gifted or culturally deprived children, teachers of adult literacy, librarians, and educational researchers.

IV. STRENGTHENING PUBLIC ELEMENTARY AND SECONDARY EDUCATION

Improved research and teacher training are not enough, if good teachers do not choose to teach. Yet present salary schedules in some cases are too low at the start to compete against other positions available to college graduates. In almost all cases, they are too low at the top to retain our ablest young teachers. Without sufficient incentive to make teaching a lifetime career, teachers with valuable training and experience but heavy family responsibilities too often become frustrated and drop out of the profession. Their children may never try to enter. Although teachers' salaries have generally improved in the Nation in recent years, there are still districts which have starting salaries below $3,000.

Good teachers, moreover, need good schools. Last year, over 1,500,000 children were in overcrowded classrooms and an estimated 2 million others were studying amid grossly substandard health and safety conditions. In many areas school dropouts, or the education of the economically disadvantaged, the culturally deprived, the physically or mentally handicapped, and the gifted require specially designed programs which simply are not available.

I am not the first, but I hope to be the last, President to be compelled to call these needless shortcomings to the Nation's attention. These are national problems crossing State boundaries, and deserving of national attention. In our mobile population—where every year one out of five families moves, sometimes across the street, but often across State lines— every family has reason to make teaching in every State a more rewarding and productive profession, and to help every State strengthen its public elementary and secondary education, particularly in those school districts that are financially unable to keep up.

Yet let us face the fact that the Federal Government cannot provide all the financial assistance needed to solve all of the problems mentioned. Instead of a general aid approach that could at best create a small wave in a huge ocean, our efforts should be selective and stimulative, encouraging the States to redouble their efforts under a plan that would phase out Federal aid over a 4-year period.

I recommend, therefore, a 4-year program to provide $1.5 billion to assist States in undertaking under their own State plans selective and urgent improvements in public elementary and secondary education including: (1) increasing starting and maximum teacher salaries, and increasing average teacher salaries in economically disdvantaged areas; (2) constructing classrooms in areas of critical and dangerous shortage; and (3) initiating pilot, experimental, or demonstration projects to meet special educational problems, particularly in slums and depressed rural and urban areas.

I also recommend extension of the National Defense Education Act programs which contribute to improving the quality of elementary and secondary education. Grants for testing, guidance, and counseling programs should be expanded and continued beyond the 1964 expiration date. This program has great relevance for the detection of incipient problems which inhibit learning and for development of the talents of our youth. National Defense Education Act assistance for science, mathematics, and foreign language laboratory equipment—which is essentially for adequate educational programs using newly developed teaching methods—should also be continued beyond 1964.

Finally, in regard to elementary and secondary schools, *I recommend a 4-year continuation of those portions of the federally affected area laws which expire June 30, 1963.* These statutes now assist some 4,000 school districts located in every State, which together enroll one-third of all public elementary and secondary school pupils in the Nation. Almost 60,000 critically needed classrooms have been constructed at a cost of $1.15 billion to house more than 1,700,000 pupils; and school operating budgets have been supplemented by more than $1.7 billion. For fiscal 1964 the present provisions would be extended. Limited modifications of the existing provisions, which would take effect beginning in 1965, would overcome certain inequities demonstrated by past experience. Also, the District of Columbia should be added to the jurisdictions eligible to participate.

V. VOCATIONAL AND SPECIAL EDUCATION

Since the wartime administration of President Woodrow Wilson, Congress has recognized the national necessity of widespread vocational education. Although revised and extended frequently since 1917, the national vocational education acts are no longer adequate. Many once-familiar occupations have declined or disappeared and wholly new industries and jobs have emerged from economic growth and change. The complexities of modern science and technology require training at a higher level than ever before.

For this reason, 2 years ago I requested the Secretary of Health, Education, and Welfare to convene an expert and representative committee to review and evaluate the present vocational education laws and to make recommendtions for their modernization. The report of that committee shows the need for providing new training opportunities—in occupations which have revelance to contemporary America—to 21 million youth now in grade school who will enter the labor market without a college degree during the 1960's. These youth—representing more than 80 percent of the population between the ages of 16 and 21—will be entering the labor market at a time when the need for unskilled labor is sharply diminishing. It is equally necessary to provide training or retraining for the millions of workers who need to learn new skills or whose skills and technical knowledge must be updated.

Both budgetary action and enactment of new legislation is called for. In my 1964 budget *I have recommended funds which would permit doubling the number of workers to be trained by the Manpower Development and Training Act programs.* These programs have, in their brief existence, already enrolled more than 18,000 men, women, and out-of-school youths who are being trained in occupations where jobs are available.

In addition, I recommend legislation to—

(*a*) *Expand the scope and level of vocational education programs supported through the Office of Education by replacing the Vocational Education Act of 1946 with new grant-in-aid legislation aimed at meeting the needs of individuals in all age groups for vocational training in occupations where they can find employment in today's diverse labor markets, and*

(*b*) *Provide employment and training opportunities for unemployed youth in conservation and local public service projects.* The details of this latter proposal are contained in a separate bill, the Youth Employment Opportunities Act, and will be discussed in a later message to be sent to the Congress.

VI. CONTINUING EDUCATION

Education need not and should not end upon graduation at any level. An increasing number of Americans recognize the need and the value of continuing education. The accountant, the salesman, the merchant, the skilled and semiskilled worker, all interested in self-improvement, should all be afforded the opportunity of securing up-to-date knowledge and skills. Only one American in eight has even taken as much as one college course. Yet the State universities and land-grant colleges which offer the majority of extension or part-time courses enroll less than a half million people. Due to inadequate finances and facilities, these colleges can offer only a very limited adult education program.

I recommend legislation authorizing Federal grants to States for expanding university extension courses in land-grant colleges and State universities. Despite our high level of educational opportunity and attainment, nearly 23 million adult Americans lack an eighth-grade education. They represent a staggering economic and cultural loss to their families and the Nation. *I recommend again, as part of this comprehensive bill, a program to assist all States in offering literacy and basic education courses to adults.*

The public library is also an important resource for continuing education. But 18 million people in this Nation still have no access to any local public library service and over 110 million more have only inadequate service.

Advanced age, lack of space, and lack of modern equipment characterize American public library buildings in 1963. Their rate of replacement is barely noticeable: 2 percent in a decade. There are now no Carnegie funds available for libraries, nor have there been for 40 years.

The public library building is usually one of the oldest governmental structures in use in any community. In one prosperous midwestern State, for example, 30 percent of all public library buildings were built before year 1910, and 85 percent were erected before 1920. Many other States are in a similar situation.

I recommend enactment of legislation to amend the Library Services Act by authorizing a 3-year program of grants for urban as well as rural libraries and for construction as well as operation.

VII. CONCLUSION

In all the years of our national life, the American people, in partnership with their governments, have continued to insist that "the means of education shall forever be encouraged," as the Continental Congress affirmed in the Northwest Ordinance. Fundamentally, education is and must always be a local responsibility, for it thrives best when nurtured at the grassroots of our democracy. But in our present era of economic expansion, population growth, and technological advance, State, local, and private efforts are insufficient. These efforts must be reinforced by national support if American education is to yield a maximum of individual development and national well-being.

The necessity of this program does not rest on the course of the cold war. Improvement in education is essential to our Nation's development without respect to what others are doing. Nevertheless, it is worthwhile noting that the Soviet Union recognizes that educational effort in the 1960's will have a major effect on a nation's power, progress, and status in the 1970's and 1980's. According to a recent report prepared for the National Science Foundation, Soviet institutions of higher education are graduating three times as many engineers and four times as many physicians as the United States. While trailing behind this country in aggregate annual numbers of higher education graduates, the Soviets are maintaining an annual flow of scientific and technical professional manpower more than twice as large as our own. At the same time, they have virtually eliminated illiteracy, with a 23-fold increase since the turn of the century in the proportion of persons with an education beyond the seventh grade. This Nation's devotion to education is surely sufficient to excel the achievements of any other nation or system.

The program here proposed is reasonable and yet far reaching. It offers Federal assistance without Federal control. It provides for economic growth, manpower development, and progress toward our educational and humanitarian objectives. It encourages the increase of the knowledge, skills, attitudes, and critical intelligence necessary for the preservation of our society. It will help keep America strong and safe and free. I strongly recommend it to the Congress for high priority action.

JOHN F. KENNEDY.

THE WHITE HOUSE, *January 29, 1963.*

Message

from

The President of the United States

Transmitting

Education Program

89th Congress, 1st Session

To the Congress of the United States:

In 1787, the Continental Congress declared in the Northwest Ordinance:

Schools and the means of education shall forever be encouraged.

America is strong and prosperous and free because for 178 years we have honored that commitment.

In the United States today—

One-quarter of all Americans are in the Nation's classrooms.

High school attendance has grown eighteenfold since the turn of the century—six times as fast as the population.

College enrollment has advanced eightyfold. Americans today support a fourth of the world's institutions of higher learning and a third of its professors and college students.

In the life of the individual, education is always an unfinished task. And in the life of this Nation, the advancement of education is a continuing challenge.

There is a darker side to education in America:

One student out of every three now in the fifth grade will drop out before finishing high school—if the present rate continues.

Almost a million young people will continue to quit school each year—if our schools fail to stimulate their desire to learn.

Over 100,000 of our brightest high school graduates each year will not go to college—and many others will leave college—if the opportunity for higher education is not expanded.

The cost of this neglect runs high—both for the youth and the Nation:

Unemployment of young people with an eighth grade education or less is four times the national average.

Jobs filled by high school graduates rose by 40 percent in the last 10 years. Jobs for those with less schooling decreased by nearly 10 percent.

We can measure the cost in even starker terms. We now spend about $450 a year per child in our public schools. But we spend $1,800 a year to keep a delinquent youth in a detention home, $2,500 a year for a family on relief, $3,500 a year for a criminal in State prison.

The growing numbers of young people reaching school age demand that we move swiftly even to stand still.

Attendance in elementary and secondary schools will increase by 4 million in the next 5 years; 400,000 new classrooms will be needed to meet this growth. But almost one-half million of the Nation's existing classrooms are already more than 30 years old.

The post-World War II boom in babies has now reached college age. And by 1970, our colleges must be prepared to add 50 percent more enrollment to their presently overcrowded facilities.

In the past, Congress has supported an increasing commitment to education in America. Last year, I signed historic measures passed by the 88th Congress to provide—

Facilities badly needed by universities, colleges, and community colleges;

Major new resources for vocational training;

More loans and fellowships for students enrolled in higher education; and

enlarged and improved training for physicians, dentists, and nurses.

I propose that the 89th Congress join me in extending the commitment still further. I propose that we declare a national goal of

FULL EDUCATIONAL OPPORTUNITY

Every child must be encouraged to get as much education as he has the ability to take.

We want this not only for his sake—but for the Nation's sake.

Nothing matters more to the future of our country: not our military preparedness, for armed might is worthless if we lack the brainpower to build a world of peace; not our productive economy, for we cannot sustain growth without trained manpower; not our democratic system of government, for freedom is fragile if citizens are ignorant.

We must demand that our schools increase not only the quantity but the quality of America's education. For we recognize that nuclear age problems cannot be solved with horse-and-buggy learning. The three R's of our school system must be supported by the three T's—teachers who are superior, techniques of instruction that are modern, and thinking about education which places it first in all our plans and hopes.

Specifically, four major tasks confront us—
>to bring better education to millions of disadvantaged youth who need it most;
>to put the best educational equipment and ideas and innovations within reach of all students;
>to advance the technology of teaching and the training of teachers; and
>to provide incentives for those who wish to learn at every stage along the road to learning.

Our program must match the magnitude of these tasks. The budget on education which I request for fiscal year 1966 will contain a total of $4.1 billion. This includes $1.1 billion to finance programs established by the 88th Congress. I will submit a request for $1.5 billion in new obligational authority to finance the programs described in this message. This expenditure is a small price to pay for developing our Nation's most priceless resource.

In all that we do, we mean to strengthen our State and community education systems. Federal assistance does not mean Federal control—as past programs have proven. The late Senator Robert Taft declared:

> Education is primarily a State function—but in the field of education, as in the fields of health, relief, and medical care, the Federal Government has a secondary obligation to see that there is a basic floor under those essential services for all adults and children in the United States.

In this spirit, I urge that we now push ahead with the No. 1 business of the American people—the education of our youth in preschools, elementary and secondary schools, and in the colleges and universities.

I. Preschool Programs

My budget will include up to $150 million for preschool projects under the community action program of the Economic Opportunity Act.

Education must begin with the very young. The child from the urban or rural slum frequently misses his chance even before he begins school. Tests show that he is usually a year behind in academic attainment by the time he reaches the third grade—and up to 3 years behind if he reaches the eighth grade. By then the handicap has grown too great for many children. Their horizons have narrowed; their prospects for lifetimes of failure have hardened. A large percentage of our young people whose family incomes are less than $2,000 do not go beyond the eighth grade.

Preschool programs have demonstrated marked success in overcoming this initial handicap:

>In New York City, children from slum neighborhoods who attended nursery school have performed better when tested in the third and fourth grades than those who did not attend.

In Baltimore, children with language and cultural handicaps are being helped greatly by a preschool program. According to preliminary reports, two-thirds of them are in the top 50 percent of their kindergarten and first grade classes on a citywide measure; one-sixth of them are in the top quarter.

But today, almost half of our school districts conduct no kindergarten classes. Public nursery schools are found in only about 100 of our 26,000 school districts. We must expand our preschool program in order to reach disadvantaged children early.

Action on a wide front will begin this summer through a special "head-start" program for children who are scheduled to begin school next fall. In addition, funds for low-income schools, regional education laboratories, and supplementary educational centers and services (recommended below) will be devoted to these vital preschool programs.

II. ELEMENTARY AND SECONDARY SCHOOLS

Elementary and secondary schools are the foundation of our education system:

Forty-eight million students are now in our grade and high schools.

Seventy-one percent of the Nation's expenditures for education are spent on elementary and secondary schooling.

If these schools are to do their job properly, they need help and they need it now. I propose that we give first priority to a program of:

A. TO LOW-INCOME SCHOOL DISTRICTS

I recommend that legislation be enacted to authorize a major program of assistance to public elementary and secondary schools serving children of low-income families. My budget for fiscal year 1966 will request $1 billion for this new program.

One hundred years ago, a man with 6 or 7 years of schooling stood well above the average. His chances to get ahead were as good as the next man's. But today, lack of formal education is likely to mean low wages, frequent unemployment, and a home in an urban or rural slum.

Poverty has many roots, but the taproot is ignorance:

Poverty is the lot of two-thirds of the families in which the family head has had 8 years or less of schooling.

20 percent of the youth aged 18 to 24 with an eighth-grade education or less are unemployed—four times the national average.

Just as ignorance breeds poverty, poverty all too often breeds ignorance in the next generation:

Nearly half the youths rejected by selective service for educational deficiency have fathers who are unemployed or else working in unskilled and low income jobs.

Fathers of more than one-half of the draft rejectees did not complete the eighth grade.

The burden on the Nation's schools is not evenly distributed. Low-income families are heavily concentrated in particular urban neighborhoods or rural areas. Faced with the largest educational needs, many of these school districts have inadequate financial resources. This imbalance has been increased by the movement of high income families from the center of cities to the suburbs—and their replacement by low-income families from rural areas:

The five States with the lowest incomes spend only an average of $276 per pupil, less than half the average of the five highest income States.

Despite a massive effort, our big cities generally spend only about two-thirds as much per pupil as their adjacent suburbs.

In our 15 largest cities, 60 percent of the 10th-grade students from poverty neighborhoods drop out before finishing high school.

This is a national problem. Federal action is needed to assist the States and localities in bringing the full benefits of education to children of low-income families.

Assistance will be provided—

on the basis of census data showing the distribution of low-income families among the counties or school districts within States.

through payments made to States for distribution to school districts.

with the assurance that the funds will be used for improving the quality of education in schools serving low-income areas.

on the condition that Federal funds will not be used to reduce State and local fiscal efforts.

for the benefit of all children within the area served, including those who participate in shared services or other special educational projects.

B. SCHOOL LIBRARY RESOURCES AND INSTRUCTIONAL MATERIALS

I recommend legislation to authorize Federal grants to States to assist in the purchase of books for school libraries and for student use, to be made available to children in public and private nonprofit elementary and secondary schools.

Thomas Carlyle once said:

All that mankind has done, thought, gained, or been: it is lying as in magic preservation in the pages of books.

Yet our school libraries are limping along:

Almost 70 percent of the public elementary schools have no

libraries; 84 percent lack librarians to teach children the value of learning through good books.

Many schools have an average of less than one-half book per child.

To meet the accepted standards for library materials would require a fourfold increase in current expenditures in our major cities.

The explosion of knowledge and the rapid revision of curriculums in the schools has created new demands for school textbooks. The obsolete text can suffocate the learning process. Yet the cost of purchasing textbooks at increasing prices puts a major obstacle in the path of education—an obstacle that can and must be eliminated.

C. SUPPLEMENTARY EDUCATIONAL CENTERS AND SERVICES

I recommend a program of Federal grants for supplementary education centers and services within the community.

We think of schools as places where youth learns, but our schools also need to learn.

The educational gap we face is one of *quality* as well as *quantity*.

Exciting experiments in education are underway, supported by the National Science Foundation, by the Office of Education, and other Government agencies, and by private philanthropic foundations. Many of our children have studied the "new" math. There are highly effective ways of teaching high school physics, biology, chemistry, and foreign languages.

We need to take full advantage of these and other innovations. Specialists can spark the interest of disadvantaged students. Remedial reading courses open up new vistas for slow learners. Gifted students can be brought along at a faster pace.

Yet such special educational services are not available in many communities. A limited local tax base cannot stand the expense. Most individual schools are not large enough to justify the services.

The supplementary center can provide such services as—

special courses in science, foreign languages, literature, music, and art.

programs for the physically handicapped and mentally retarded.

instruction in the sciences and humanities during the summer for economically and culturally deprived children.

special assistance after regular school hours.

common facilities that can be maintained more efficiently for a group of schools than for a single school—laboratories, libraries, auditoriums, and theaters.

a system by which gifted persons can teach part time to provide scarce talents.

a means of introducing into the school system new courses, instructional materials, and teaching practices.

a way of tapping the community's extracurricular resources for the benefit of students—museums, concert and lecture programs, and industrial laboratories.

Within each community, public and private nonprofit schools and agencies will cooperate to devise the plan and administer the program for these supplementary centers. Their services should be adapted to meet the pressing needs of each locality.

D. REGIONAL EDUCATION LABORATORIES

I recommend the establishment under the Cooperative Research Act of regional educational laboratories which will undertake research, train teachers, and implement tested research findings.

I further recommend amendments to the act to—

broaden the types of research organizations now eligible for educational projects.

train educational research personnel.

provide grants for research, development of new curriculums, dissemination of information, and implementation of educational innovations.

support construction of research facilities and the purchase of research equipment.

Under auspices of the National Science Foundation, educators have worked with scientists—including Nobel laureates—to develop courses which capture the excitement of contemporary science. They have prepared totally new instructional materials—laboratory equipment, textbooks, teachers' guides, films, supplementary reading, and examinations. After testing, they are made available to public and private schools.

We need to extend our research and development to history, literature, and economics; to art and music; to reading, writing, and speaking; to occupational, vocational, and technical education. We need to extend it to all stages of learning—preschool, elementary and secondary schools, college and graduate training.

Regional laboratories for education offer great promise. They draw equally upon educators and the practitioners in all fields of learning— mathematicians, scientists, social scientists, linguists, musicians, artists, and writers. They help both to improve curriculums and to train teachers.

E. STRENGTHENING STATE EDUCATIONAL AGENCIES

I recommend a program of grants to State educational agencies.

State leadership becomes increasingly important as we seek to improve the quality of elementary and secondary education.

We should assist the States by strengthening State departments of education in their efforts to—
>   Provide consultative and technical assistance for local school districts and local school leadership.
>   Formulate long-range plans.
>   Expand educational research and development.
>   Improve local and State information about education.
>   Identify emerging educational problems.
>   Provide for the training of State and local education personnel.
>   Conduct periodic evaluation of educational programs.
>   Promote teacher improvement courses.

* * *

These new programs will substantially augment community resources in the war against poverty. As provided by sections 611 and 612 of the Economic Opportunity Act of 1964, I will see that the new efforts are kept in step with our other antipoverty efforts.

In those localities where the community has undertaken a community action program under the Economic Opportunity Act, the community agency should participate in the planning of these new educational programs and in their coordination with ongoing and developing antipoverty efforts.

* * *

Enactment of these proposals for elementary and secondary education is of utmost urgency. I urge early and favorable consideration by the Congress.

III. HIGHER EDUCATION

Higher education is no longer a luxury, but a necessity.

Programs enacted by Congress in the past have contributed greatly to strengthening our colleges and universities. These will be carried forward under my 1966 budget, which includes—
>   An additional $179 million to assist construction of college classrooms, libraries, and laboratories.
>   An additional $25 million for 4,500 more graduate fellowships to overcome college teaching shortages.
>   An additional $110 million to further basic research in the universities, to provide science fellowships, and to promote science education.

But we need to do more:
>   To extend the opportunity for higher education more broadly among lower and middle income families.
>   To help small and less well developed colleges improve their programs.

To enrich the library resources of colleges and universities.

To draw upon the unique and invaluable resources of our great universities to deal with national problems of poverty and community development.

A. ASSISTANCE TO STUDENTS

1. *Scholarships.—*

I recommend a program of scholarships for needy and qualified high school graduates to enable them to enter and to continue in college.

Loans authorized by the National Defense Education Act currently assist nearly 300,000 college students. Still the following conditions exist:

Each year an estimated 100,000 young people of demonstrated ability fail to go on to college because of lack of money. Many thousands more from low-income families must borrow heavily to meet college costs.

Only one out tof three young people from *low*-income families attend college compared with four out of five from *high*-income families.

For many young people from poor families loans are not enough to open the way to higher education.

Under this program, a special effort will be made to identify needy students of promise early in their high school careers. The scholarship will serve as a building block, to be augmented by work-study and other support, so that the needy student can chart his own course in higher studies.

My 1966 budget provides sufficient funds for grants to help up to 140,000 students in the first year.

2. *Expansion of work-study opportunity and guaranteed low-interest loans.—*

I recommend—

That the existing college work-study program be made available to more students and that authority for the program be transferred to the Department of Health, Education, and Welfare.

That a part of the cost of interest payments on guaranteed private loans to college students be paid by the Federal Government.

Going to college is increasingly expensive. A student must pay nearly $2,400 a year in a private college and about $1,600 in a public college. These costs may rise by one-third over the next decade.

Two aids should be extended to meet the heavy costs of college education. First, the existing work-study program should be expanded for students from low-income families and extended to students from middle-income families. Under this program the Federal Government pays 90 percent of the wages earned by students on useful projects.

This will enable a student to earn on the average of $450 during a school year, and up to $500 more during the summer.

Second, many families cannot cover all of college expenses on an out-of-pocket basis. We should assure greater availability of private credit on reasonable terms and conditions. This can best be done by paying part of interest cost of guaranteed loans made by private lenders —a more effective, fairer, and far less costly way of providing assistance than the various tax credit devices which have been proposed.

B. AID TO SMALLER COLLEGES

I recommend that legislation be enacted to strengthen less developed colleges.

Many of our smaller colleges are battling for survival. About 10 percent lack proper accreditation, and others face constantly the threat of losing accreditation. Many are isolated from the main currents of academic life.

Private sources and States alone cannot carry the whole burden of doing what must be done for these important units in our total educational system. Federal aid is essential.

Universities should be encouraged to enter into cooperative relationships to help less developed colleges, including such assistance as—

A program of faculty exchanges.

Special programs to enable faculty members of small colleges to renew and extend knowledge of their fields.

A national fellowship program to encourage highly qualified young graduate students and instructors in large universities to augment the teaching resources of small colleges.

The development of joint programs to make more efficient use of available facilities and faculty.

In union there is strength. This is the basic premise of my recommendation.

C. MORE SUPPORT FOR COLLEGE LIBRARY RESOURCES

I recommend enactment of legislation for purchase of books and library materials to strengthen college teaching and research.

Fifty percent of our 4-year institutions and 82 percent of our 2-year institutions fall below accepted professional standards in the number of volumes possessed.

As student enrollment mounts, we must look not only to the physical growth of our colleges and universities. They must be developed as true centers of intellectual activity. To construct a library building is meaningless unless there are books to bring life to the library.

D. UNIVERSITY-COMMUNITY EXTENSION PROGRAM

I recommend a program of grants to support university extension concentrating on problems of the community.

Institutions of higher learning are being called on ever more frequently for public service—for defense research, foreign development, and countless other programs. They have performed magnificently. We must now call upon them to meet new needs.

Once 90 percent of our population earned its living from the land. A wise Congress enacted the Morrill Act of 1862 and the Hatch Act of 1887 which helped the State universities help the American people. With the aid of the land-grant colleges, American agriculture produced overwhelming abundance.

Today, 70 percent of our people live in urban communities. They are confronted by problems of poverty, residential blight, polluted air and water, inadequate mass transportation and health services, strained human relations, and overburdened municipal services.

Our great universities have the skills and knowledge to match these mountainous problems. They can offer expert guidance in community planning; research and development in pressing educational problems; economic and job market studies; continuing education of the community's professional and business leadership; and programs for the disadvantaged.

The role of the university must extend far beyond the ordinary extension-type operation. Its research findings and talents must be made available to the community. Faculty must be called upon for consulting activities. Pilot projects, seminars, conferences, TV programs, and task forces drawing on many departments of the university—all should be brought into play.

This is a demanding assignment for the universities, and many are not now ready for it. The time has come for us to help the university to face problems of the city as it once faced problems of the farm.

E. SPECIAL MANPOWER NEEDS

We must also ask the colleges and universities to help overcome certain acute deficiencies in trained manpower. At least 100,000 more professional librarians are needed for service in public libraries and in schools and colleges. We need 140,000 more teachers for handicapped children.

I recommend:

Grants to institutions of higher education for training of school, college, and community librarians and related services.

Extension and expansion of grants for training teachers and handicapped children.

CONCLUSION

In 1838, Mirabeau B. Lamar, the second President of the Republic of Texas and the father of Texas education, declared:

The cultivated mind is the guardian genius of democracy. It is the only dictator that freeman acknowledges. It is the only security that freeman desires.

Throughout the history of our Nation, the United States has recognized this truth. But during the periods when the country has been most astir with creative activity, when it most keenly sensed the sturdiness of the old reaching out for the vigor of the new, it has given special attention to its educational system.

This was true in the expansive 1820's and 1830's, when the American people acted decisively to build a public school system for the lower grades. It was no less true at the vigorous turn of the 20th century, when high schools were developed for the millions. Again, during the questing 1930's, fresh ideas stirred the traditions of the ruler and blackboard.

We are now embarked on another venture to put the American dream to work in meeting the new demands of a new day. Once again we must start where men who would improve their society have always known they must begin—with an educational system restudied, reinforced, and revitalized.

LYNDON B. JOHNSON.

THE WHITE HOUSE, *January 12, 1965.*

Appendix B]

Elementary and Secondary Education
Act of 1965
(Public Law 89–10)

Title I—Education of Children of Low Income Families F.Y. 1966—$775 million. Designed to encourage and support the establishment, expansion, and improvement of special programs, including the construction of school facilities where needed, to meet the special needs of educationally deprived children of low income families. Public school districts are eligible for payments for programs designed to meet the special educational needs of children in school attendance areas having high concentrations of disadvantaged children. In these areas, the school district designs special educational services and arrangements, including those in which all children in need of such services may participate. These special programs include dual enrollment (shared services), educational radio and television, mobile educational services and equipment, remedial education, preschool or after-school programs, additional instructional personnel, equipment and facilities, and others judged necessary for improving the education of disadvantaged children. Local educational agencies are eligible for payments equal to one-half the average per-pupil expenditure in that State multiplied by (a) the number of children (aged 5-17) in families having an annual income of less than $2,000; and (b) the number of children in families receiving payments over $2,000 under the program of Aid to Families with Dependent Children. State and local educational effort must be maintained.

Title II—School Library Resources, Textbooks, and Other Instructional Materials F.Y. 1966—$100 million. A 5-year program to make available for the use of school children school library resources and other printed and published instructional materials including textbooks. State plans must provide for a method of making available materials for the use of all school children in the State. Title to all of these materials and control and administration of their use must be vested only in a public agency. Materials purchased with Federal funds must, when made available for use of students in non-public schools, be the same as those used or approved for use in the public schools of the State.

Title III—Supplementary Educational Centers and Services F.Y. 1966 —$75 million. A 5-year program to provide vitally needed educational services not available in sufficient quantity or quality in elementary and secondary schools and to develop and establish exemplary and innovative elementary and secondary school educational programs to serve as models for regular school programs. Special personnel, equipment, and other costly educational services not normally available in most schools are made available in centers for the widest possible participation of the entire community.

Title IV—Educational Research and Training; Cooperative Research Act F.Y. 1966—$70 million. Authorizes the training of research personnel and improved dissemination of information derived from educational research development. Authority is granted to utilize the research competence of research organizations not now eligible to contribute to the program, such as private non-collegiate research organizations and professional associations. In addition, the program provides for the construction and operation of research facilities to improve the quality of teaching in our schools and for the purchase of research equipment.

Title V—State Departments of Education F.Y. 1966—$17 million. A 5-year program to stimulate and assist in strengthening the leadership resources of State educational agencies. The State educational agency identifies educational needs of the State and designs programs to meet these needs.

Index